More Oats

Sam Ed Spence

Cover: *Bringing In The Hay* by John F. Herring, Jr.

Edited by John Records and Diane Waldon

Design and layout by Ken Fraser

Race Track Chaplaincy of Texas
1000 Lone Star Parkway
Grand Prairie, Texas 75050
(972) 237-4818
www.racetrackchaplaincytexas.org

God is love.

"Love never fails, His mercies never cease. Everything about God is forever. He never changes....what you think about God is the most important thought you will ever have."

Graham Cooke

Are you ready? Set your hat down, take a deep seat in the saddle, "or sofa," and get ready for an awesome ride. In *More Oats*, my lifelong friend, Sam Ed Spence, is anointed to take you on a journey into the heart of God. You may encounter new levels or see some familiar places in a brand new light. One thing is for sure, you will be touched by his love.

> **—Jeff Copenhaver, former world champion calf roper, pastor of the original cowboy church, Fort Worth, TX, and founder of The Master's Champions ministry.**

About ten years ago we began running a page each month in our magazine that contained a single devotional. It quickly became the most popular article in the magazine. I can hardly wait for our readers to get *More Oats*.

> **— Ben Hudson, editor-publisher, *Track magazine*.**

Wow! Praise the Lord. . . Chaplain Sam's talent for writing, combined with the accompanying magnificent artistry makes *More Oats* a beautiful work of God. Thanks to Sam's spiritual insight and perseverance, the reader will be led into a deeper relationship with our Lord and Savior, Jesus Christ.

> **— Chaplain Craig N. Wiley, executive director, Race Track Chaplaincy of America.**

Race track Chaplain Sam Ed Spence combines a lifetime of experience with horses, a knack for the vernacular of the track and a personal relationship with the Son of God in these brief but powerful devotionals that lift even as they instruct.

> **— Henry King, founding editor-publisher of *Lone Star Horse Report*.**

Our world doesn't let us gather much thinking time, but it's how in our thought lives where God nurtures us. *More Oats* gave me a lot to think about, and I found myself – once again – listening to a Holy God.

> **— Billy Smith, executive director, American Paint Horse Assn.**

Reading *More Oats* was like sitting before a warm fire on a cold night with a steaming cup of tea. The pictures are heartwarming and bring the message home with love and a gentle grace. God's love shone from every page, and in a easy way, much like a conversation with a wise old friend that even the newest of believers can understand and learn from. God's love is available to everyone, and *More Oats* brings that message home in a way that is reachable, believable, and understandable.

> **— Courtney Diehl, DVM, author of *Horse Vet*.**

More Oats

ISBN 3: 978-0-578-13714-8

Printed in USA
Health Communications, Inc.
Deerfield Beach, FL

©2014 by Sam Ed Spence

Race Track Chaplaincy of Texas*
1000 Lone Star Parkway
Grand Prairie, TX 75050

*An affiliate of:
Race Track Chaplaincy of America
www.rtcanational.org

Cover and text art designed by Ken Fraser, www.grafxedge.com

Art Credits

Our special thanks and sincere appreciation to the following artists who have graciously allowed us to reproduce their work in this volume. Prints of most of these paintings can be ordered from the individual artists.

Tom Chapman, Redwood City, CA, 650/369-1823, www.chapman-arts.com; tchapman@jps.net. *Faithful and True* (Day 2); *Fit for a King* (Day 31); *RTCA—God's Hands* (Day 46); *Down the Stretch They Come* (Day 47); *Barnward Bound* (Day 58).

Tim Cox, Bloomfield, NM, 505/632-8080, www.timcox.com. *Reflections on a Passing Day* (Day 8); *A Helping Hand* (Day 9); *Little Boys Dream the Biggest Dreams* (Day 23); *Between Heaven and Earth* (Day 25); *Another Day Gone* (Day 35); *Quiet Time* (Day 37); *Quality Time* (Day 43); *A Lot Like Heaven* (Day 44); *Straight from the Well* (Day 50); *Where Freedom Lives* (Day 56).

Chuck DeHaan, Graford, TX, 940/329-9911, www.chuckdehaan.com. *The Quarter Horse* (Day 3); *Above and Beyond* (Day 4); *Waiting for the Master* (Day 6); *Clearview* (Day 11); *Whoa!* (Day 12); *Raising Snow Dust* (Day 14); *Spring Break* (Day 15); *Spirit Wind* (Day 16); *Eye of Freedom* (Day 17); *Adios Cowboy* (Day 19); *72 Degrees in Amarillo, Yesterday* (Day 20); *Eyes of Autumn* (Day 21); *Sunset Surprise* (Day 22); *Prairie Storm* (Day 24); *Water Breaking* (Day 26); *Boss Hoss* (Day 27); *First Touch of Morning* (Day 28); *Freedom* (Day 29); *Two Horses* (Day 32); *Mare and Young at River* (Day 33); *Cross Roads* (Day 34); *Lost and Found and Lost* (Day 36); *Cattle Baron* (Day 38); *Goosed* (Day 39); *Moonlight* (Day 40); *Escape* (Day 41); *Stable at Night* (Day 42); *In the Early Years* (Day 48); *Roping!* (Day 49); *Winter Renegade* (day 51); *The Searchers* (Day 52); *Paint in the Mist* (Day 53); *Blizzard Peril* (Day 54); *In Search of Buffalo* (Day 55); *Cutting Horse* (Day 59); *The Winner* (Day 60).

Fred Fellows, Sonoita, AZ, 520/455-5010, www.fellowsstudios.com. *Friends for Supper* (Day 5); *Driving in the Fast Lane* (Day 45).

Russell Houston, Edgar AZ, 800/776-1594, www.russellhouston.com. *Whiff* (Day 7); *Sudden Death* (Day 30).

Jack Sorenson, Amarillo, TX, sorensonart@gmail.com. Rich Wiseman, LLC, 505/466-1927. *The Thinker* (Day 1); *The Good Book* (Day 10); *Down from the High Country* (Day 13); *The Jitters* (Day 18); *Shallow Crossing* (Day 57).

Dedication

*This book is dedicated to our ten grand-
children and one great granddaughter,
who range from twenty-three to three
years of age. They are the source of many
smiles and a world of wonderment –
blessings in our lives.*

Wesley Wayne Coleman
Madison Jane Coleman
Taylor Marie Coleman
Paisley Nicole Spence
Abbie Alexandria Timm
Zane Samuel Spence
Zachary David Spence
Kai Isabella Spence
Sienna Meryn Kingsbury
Remi Kayln Kingsbury
Kaylynn Nicole Spence

Introduction

More Oats is a continuation of our original devotional, *Daily Oats*, which was first published in 2006, followed by additional printings in 2007 and 2012.

While devotionals are never intended to replace or be a substitute for God's Word in our lives, they can sometimes serve as incentive to study the Word, search out the Creator's perfect will for our lives, and seek out the wonderful treasures of the Father's character.

Contrary to a great deal of religion, God is not boring, mundane, or redundant. Instead, He is exciting, refreshing, and has a tremendous sense of humor. His qualities of unconditional love and endless mercy are matched only by His pursuit of His greatest joy – quality time with His children, you and me.

May these pages be an assist to you in cooperating with the Father's pursuit.

Sam Ed Spence

The Thinker
Jack Sorenson

What if...

*Jesus said to him, "If you can believe, all things are possible to him who believes." **Mark 9:23***

Wh*at if...* God Almighty, the Creator of the universe, had designed a life of health, success, prosperity and peace for you from the beginning of time?

What if... this Creator loves you unconditionally and holds absolutely nothing against you?

What if... this loving God had a deep, yearning desire to have a very close, personal relationship with you that involves daily conversations and exchanges on a "best friend" basis?

What if... this same God put no performance standards and no rigid system of rules and regulations as prerequisites to qualify you for all of the above?

What if... God simply said, "I sent my Son, Jesus the Christ, to handle all of the above for you; all you have to do is believe it, and accept Him in your heart!"

"But, Chaplain, that's just too simple...too easy!"

Simple, yes, but perhaps not so easy for most of us because of religion, tradition, and maybe some angry preachers in our past. You see, the Gospel is called "Good News." In fact, some people who have done a deep study of the original language of the New Testament tell us that the literal translation of the word "gospel" is the-almost-too-good-to-be-true news. And it really is!

We simply need to read the Bible for ourselves and find out what God is really like and how He truly feels about us. Keep in mind as you read the New Testament that Jesus said He only did and said what the Father did and said. In other words, Jesus (who was 100 percent man and called Himself the "Son of Man,") was the spittin' image of Father God. Note that Jesus operated in total love…He went about doing good – healing, curing, forgiving, raising the dead, and providing what was lacking in folks' lives.
Their part – in order to receive these blessings – was simply to believe.

It's the same today. All we have to do is believe that Jesus went to that cross and actually became our sin, then went Himself into hell and paid the price for all our blown turns. Once we wade through the religion and traditions that erroneously tell us we have to somehow earn this favor with our Creator, a most wonderful thing happens…the Bible calls it being "born again." Sorta like writing a check on an account full of funds that were there all the time!

To not accept and take advantage of this love of God is comparable to having a great stakes horse in your possession, but never going to the entry booth with him!

We simply need to
read the Bible for
ourselves and find
out what God is really
like and how He truly
feels about us.

Faithful & True
Tom Chapman

Father of Lights

Every good gift and every perfect gift is from above, and comes down from the Father of lights, with whom there is no variation or shadow of turning. **James 1:17**

Few scriptures are more revealing of the true nature and character of God than this one penned by the Apostle James in his letter to the twelve tribes, those Jewish believers who had been scattered throughout the known world via the persecution in Israel.

James, the natural (and spiritual) brother of Jesus, gives us practical, "where-the-rubber-meets-the-road" instructions on life. And he wants to make absolutely sure that we understand that every blessing comes from Father God . . . that He never sends anything else! Nor will He ever send anything but blessings in this dispensation, because there's not even a hint of change in Him.

Getting this vital information settled in your heart is a big key to avoiding the doubt and double-mindedness that prevents us from receiving wisdom from God, as James points out: "If any of you lacks wisdom, let him ask of God, who gives to all liberally and without reproach, and it will be given to him. But let him ask in faith, with no doubting, for he who doubts is like a wave of the sea driven and tossed by the wind. For let not that man suppose that he will receive anything from the Lord; he is a double-minded man, unstable in all his ways." *(James 1: 5-8)*

Remember, God is the Father of lights – there is no darkness in Him.

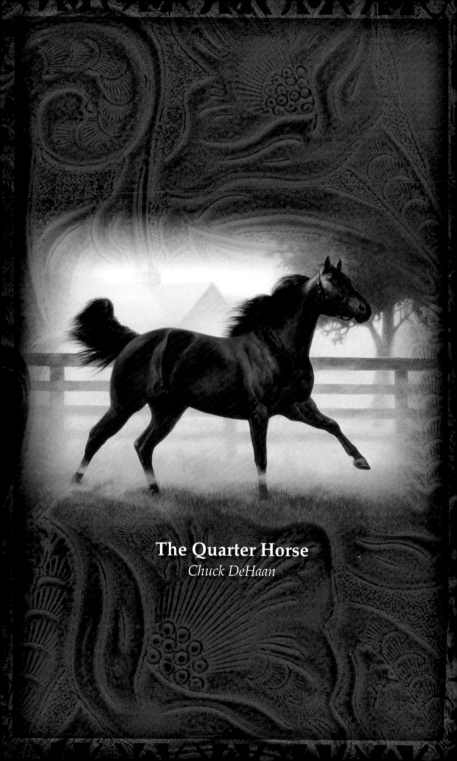

The Quarter Horse
Chuck DeHaan

A Good Worming

So then faith comes by hearing, and hearing by the
word of God. **Romans 10:17**

N ow and then you'll have a horse that doesn't shed
off his winter coat as fast as he should, or maybe
he's just not as perky as he needs to be. Chances are
pretty good that this horse needs a good worming.
He's probably got those old parasites on the inside of
him that are interfering with his various systems and
preventing him from achieving his true potential. So,
you go to the store and buy a syringe of wormer, or
you have the vet "tube him." And pretty soon, that old
pony is back on track.

Not too long ago I found myself going through some
"mullygrubbs." There were some circumstances not
lining up like I wanted them to, and I was letting them
give me an attitude. In fact, my wife informed me that
I (with my long face) was not much fun to be around.
Her comment didn't help any, but at least I decided to
go to the Lord with my problem.

On the way to the track the next morning, He came
through loud and clear: "Sam, you just need a good
worming!" He immediately showed me the parasites
on my insides that were robbing me of my joy, peace,
faith, and ultimate success. Doubt, unbelief, worry,

and concern were eating away at me. I was a prime candidate for a good tubing with God's Word!

When I got to the office, I immediately repented and got out my Bible. Incidentally, repent simply means "changing the way you think in order to go in a different direction." I realized I hadn't been in the Word much lately, and was immediately impressed to go to Romans and read our lead scripture above.

Sometimes you can be familiar with a passage, but don't know exactly where it is in the Bible. I was needing a good dose of joy, so I went to the concordance and found *Nehemiah 8:12* . . . "for the joy of the Lord is your strength." I chewed on (meditated) these verses off and on throughout the morning. In fact, I'm sure some of the backside thought the chaplain had gone plumb senile between the shedrows and was talking to himself (which I was).

But it worked. By the end of the day I did not have one mullygrub to contend with, and a smile began to work its way into my countenance, which my wife even noticed when I got home. And, amazingly, the adverse circumstances began to change within two days of my "positive meditation" . . . all because of a good worming.

For the joy of
the Lord is your
strength.

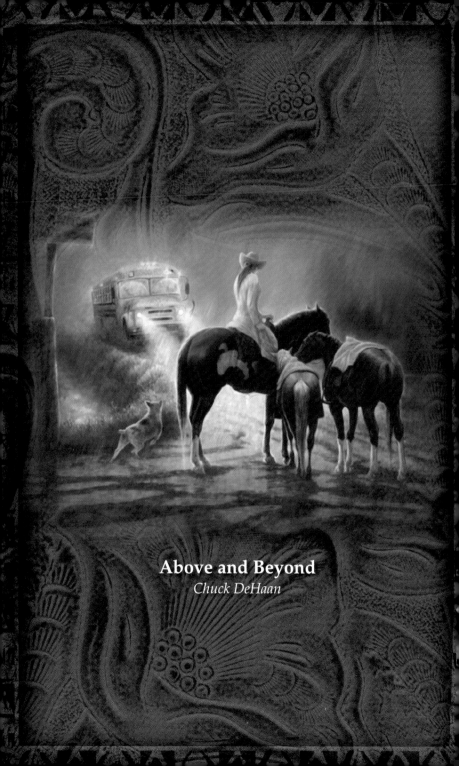

Above and Beyond
Chuck DeHaan

God's Kind of Love

"For God so loved the world that He gave his only begotten Son, that whoever believes in Him should not perish but have everlasting life." **John 3:16**

We use the word *love* to describe an array of feelings and subjects . . . all the way from our passion for peanut butter to a deep emotion about a mate for life. Possibly more songs have been written about love than any other subject. "Love is a Many Splendor Thing" is one that comes to mind; yet very few of these songs, or definitions, come close to the Greek word for love, which is used in the Bible – *agape*, the God kind of love.

It's a love that's all giving, as our scripture above so exemplifies. It's a love without strings attached. It's a love that keeps no record of wrongs and shortcomings. It's a love of second chances, and thirds, and fourths, etc., etc. It's a love that accepts you exactly as you are, but is never willing to leave you that way. It's a love that never manipulates or controls; it manifests by invitation only – yours or someone praying *for* you.

A literal translation of *agape* means: to value, hold in high regard, and consider precious. (This is exactly how God feels about you!)

God's love is all this, as well as being the most powerful force in the universe.

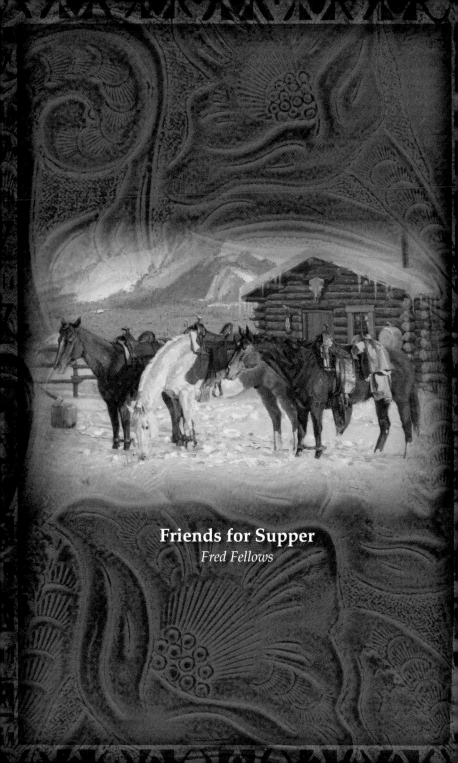

Friends for Supper
Fred Fellows

Charging the Battery

"No longer do I call you servants, for a servant does not know what his master is doing; but I have called you friends, for all things that I heard from My Father I have made known to you." **John 15:15**

My cell phone has these little bars which indicate how much juice my battery has. And when the bars disappear altogether, I get this little bleeping sound which means "low battery, time to recharge"… if I want this gismo to continue working for me.

My soul – the mind, will and emotions-part of me – operates very similar to my cell phone. Yes, I do need six-eight hours of sleep each night, but more importantly my soul needs a daily dose of being plugged into the main power source – namely, time with my Abba Father – "Daddy God," as my wife often lovingly refers to Him. And more often than not, I'm liable to need that plug-in multiple times in a 12-14-hour day's span.

If it was important for Jesus, the Son of God, to spend daily time in prayer (and the Bible tells us it was very important for Him), then daily prayer time has to be vital for you and me. I hesitate to call that "prayer time" because religion and tradition often relegates prayer to when you're asking or petitioning God for something. For most of us growing up in a Christian atmosphere, prayer was something you did before you ate, went to bed, or needed when you got in a jam. A number of years ago, however, I discovered that the Lord was more than my Creator, Savior, and get-out-of-jams Need Meeter. He was, and is, truly my best Friend.

Now, getting back to that plug-in time, think about a recent time you have had with a good friend. There was conversation, and it involved talking and listening. When I discovered God as a friend, my prayer time became more like share time. And, amazingly, my want-list became more like a thank-you list. Consequently, my soul battery started getting charged faster . . . and lasting longer.

The signals of a low soul battery are doubt, anxiety, confusion, anger, or fear. Whenever the least little hints of these *unbelief* signs crop up in your soul, it's time to immediately pull aside, get quiet, and plug into the Holy Spirit – that portable power source that resides on the inside of you.

Don't allow your soul battery to run out of juice.

...daily prayer time
has to be vital for
you and me.

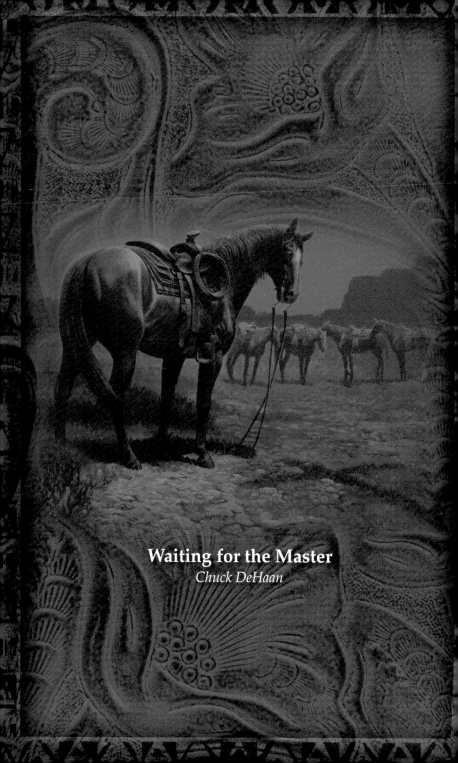

Waiting for the Master
Chuck DeHaan

Obedient to the Master

"If you are willing and obedient, you shall eat the good of the land;" **Isaiah 1:19**

There was a time in my life when I believed that to do God's will would take most all of the fun out of living. And I think that is a misconception harbored by many in the world – and even some Christians – today. Almost the exact opposite is the real truth.

When you are walking in God's perfect will for your life – obedient to His plan and directions – the real joy of living springs forth. Trials and tribulations? Yes, they still come; Jesus said they would *(John 16:33)*, but in His name you overcome and walk right through them.

Understand that the Father wants the very best for you. So don't shy away from what He speaks to you in His Word and in your heart. Know that your obedience to Him in this area is part of the plan that leads to your eating the good of the land.

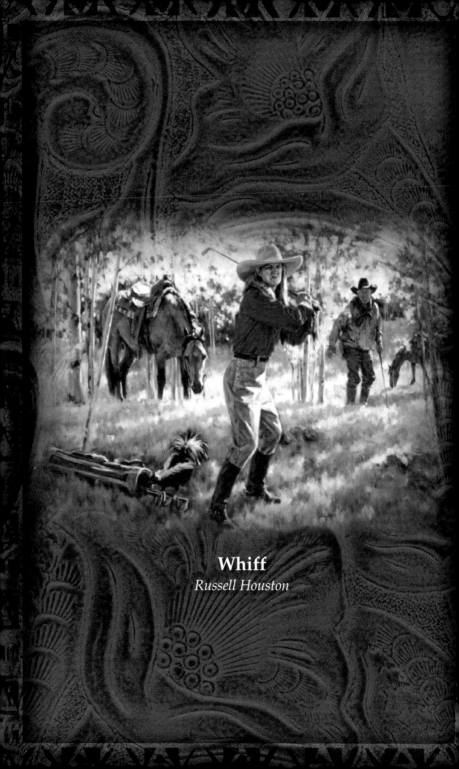

Whiff

Russell Houston

Emotions

Be anxious for nothing, but in everything by prayer and supplication, with thanksgiving, let your requests be made known to God. **Philippians 4:6**

I've found that many of the wrong or negative decisions I've made in my life came about during a strong emotional state. Noah Webster defines emotion as "a moving of the mind or soul; hence, any agitation of mind or excitement of sensibility."

We know that God gave us emotions and that we are created in His image. Jesus certainly had emotions of sadness – he cried; of anger, when he made the whip and drove the money-changers out of the temple; He had great emotions of compassion as he healed those who came to Him. He also exhibited an emotion of sadness when he lamented over Jerusalem *(Matthew 23:37)*.

Yet, in the midst of all these emotions, Jesus never sinned or missed the mark! That's because He was in control of His emotions . . . He did not allow the emotions to control Him. And remember, He was not handling this because He was the Son of God; He did it as a man, just like you and me. That tells me that we can be in control of our emotions just as was Jesus.

If you're an easily excitable person or above-the-norm (whatever that is) emotional individual, I can tell you from experience, there's help available via God's

Word. No, I haven't arrived yet, but I have left the station. This very day that I'm penning this, I let a silly emotion of impatience take hold of me at the house before I left for the track. My improper reaction to a short, meaningless delay left my spouse feeling that her dilemma was of little importance to me, compared to my busy schedule (which really didn't exist)! When I let that impatient emotion control me, I hurt the love of my life.

The greatest tool we have to control our emotions is simply "the name of Jesus." Now, this takes some practice, but start getting in the habit of speaking to your out-of-control emotions when they raise their ugly head . . . "in Jesus' name, emotion (of anger, lust, impatience, etc.), you will not control me!"

Using Jesus' name is most effective when you can speak it out loud, but you'll probably find that most times it will have to be under your breath . . . otherwise, those in hearing distance may consider you a prime candidate for the funny farm (which really doesn't matter).

God's Word is also a tremendous help in those temptable times of passion. "I can do all things through Christ who strengthens me," *(Philippians 4:13)* is a dandy to quote on the spot!

But the all-time best way to overcome any temptation (which I should have done this morning) is to simply pray, "Jesus, help me!" He does it every time.

The greatest tool
we have to control
our emotions is
simply "the name
of Jesus."

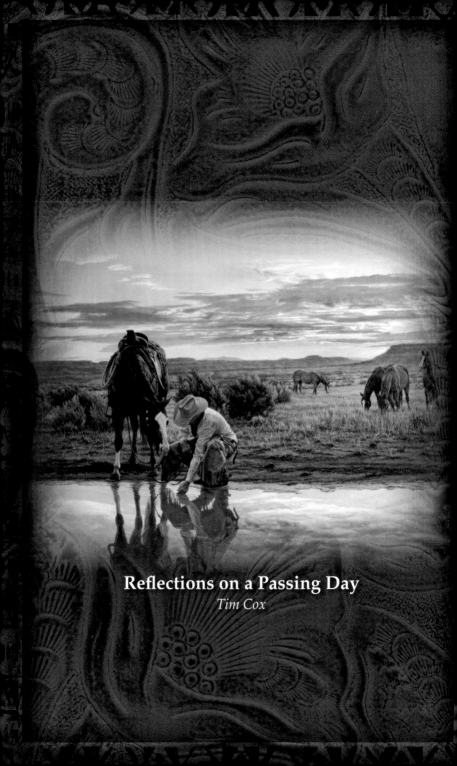

Reflections on a Passing Day
Tim Cox

Are you aware...?

But God demonstrates His own love toward us, in that while we were still sinners, Christ died for us.
Romans 5:8

It was May, 1977, and the flight was almost full as I eased into my short-row aisle seat on a trip out of DFW to Louisville, Kentucky. Seated next to me, by the window, was a middle-aged gentleman in a white knit shirt and blue sport coat. Shortly after we were airborne, he struck up a conversation, asking me where I was headed and what type of work I did.

I responded by telling him I worked for a horse racing organization and was headed to a horse sale in Kentucky. Somehow, our lengthy conversation got around to church and religion, and that's when he popped the big question to me:

"Are you aware of how much God really loves you?" His piercing blue eyes left little doubt of the sincerity of his statement, which caused me to pause and ponder. My first thoughts were to share my experience of being saved as a teenager, leaving Jesus in east Texas when I went off to college and then coming back to Him as a 34-year-old backslider, along with some deep theology I had accumulated over the past couple of years. Somehow, none of that really fit. Finally, I responded, "Probably not."

His smile seemed to say, "I appreciate your honesty;" then he said, "I'm not going to preach to you, but I do want to share a passage of scripture for you to think about." At that moment, I realized we had not only landed, but were at the gate; most everyone on board was jumping to their feet to grab their overhead baggage and get off the plane.

"It's in the eighth chapter of Romans, verses 38 and 39," said my new friend in almost a whisper just above the noise and commotion around us. He stayed seated while I hurried down the aisle and off the plane to meet someone waiting to whisk me off to a close appointment.

There really wasn't time for him to quote the Word to me, and since I never carried a Bible with me in those days, I had to wait until I was in the hotel room that night to pull out the Apostle Paul's quote in the Gideon edition. It read: "For I am persuaded that neither death nor life, nor angels nor principalities nor powers, nor things present nor things to come, nor height nor depth, nor any other created thing, shall be able to separate us from the love of God which is in Christ Jesus our Lord."

For the life of me, I can't remember the man's name, nor what kind of work he did; it seemed like we simply talked about me. Reflecting back on it many times since, I've come to the conclusion that he was a *plant* – simply an angel that was sent to deliver a message that was very important to me and many, many other people in our individual lives.

How wonderful God is, even in the midst of all our busyness, our mistakes, and our blown turns . . . He loves each of us so very much.

Are you aware
of how much God
really loves you?

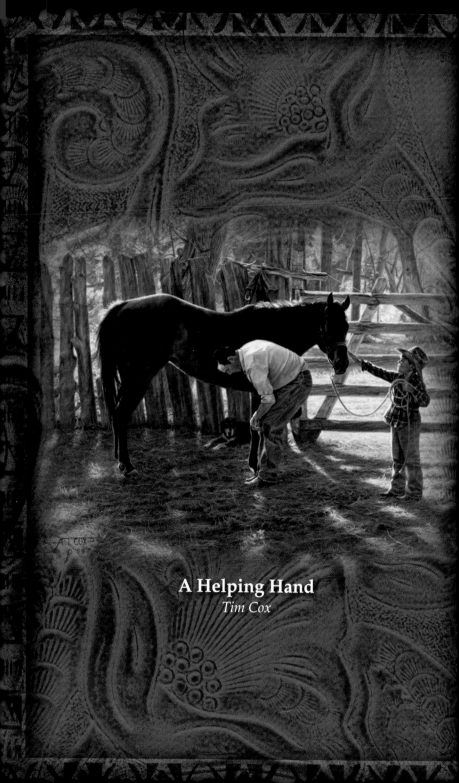

A Helping Hand
Tim Cox

Properly Shod

Therefore take up the whole armor of God, that you may be able to withstand in the evil day, and having done all, to stand . . . and having shod your feet with the preparation of the gospel of peace.
Ephesians 6:13, 15

No trainer would consider sending a horse to the gate that was not properly shod with a good set of racing plates.

Likewise, a Christian must have his or her "feet (shod) with the preparation of the gospel of peace" in order to be effective in standing against the wiles of the devil. *(Ephesians 6:11)*

It's vital for us to understand that the gospel of peace refers to you and me having perfect peace with God. We became recipients of that peace when Jesus went to the cross and was raised from the dead. Because of what Jesus accomplished for us in His substitutional sacrifice, God is not mad or upset with us in any shape, form or fashion . . . those who believe this and accept Jesus in their hearts, will never experience the wrath of God. This is exactly what the Apostle Paul is telling us in *Romans 5:8-9*, "But God demonstrates His own love toward us, in that while we were still sinners, Christ died for us. Much more then, having now been justified by His blood, we shall be saved from wrath through Him."

When Jesus was born, the angels announced "…
And on earth, peace, goodwill toward men!" *(Luke 2:14)* That is peace between God and man for all those who would accept the salvation of Jesus Christ. That scripture does not refer to peace between or among men; that kind of peace will not come until the next dispensation (1,000-year millennial reign) is ushered in when Jesus returns.

The feet of a horse are his foundation; hence the importance of him being properly shod. Understanding this peace relationship we have with our heavenly Father is foundational as we stand against the accusations of the devil (the accuser of the brethren) in our individual walks of faith. The devil absolutely does not want you and me to have a handle on the peace we have with God, and the perfect peace that is so available for us to walk in daily.

Keep in mind, "There is therefore now no condemnation to those who are in (belong to) Christ Jesus." *(Romans 8:1)* Even when you blow a turn, God's not mad at you. Jesus simply picks you up, dusts you off, and says, "It's alright, son, I paid for that, too; now let's go win the next one!" Getting this in your heart is being properly shod.

It's vital for us to
understand that
the gospel of peace
refers to you and me
having perfect peace
with God.

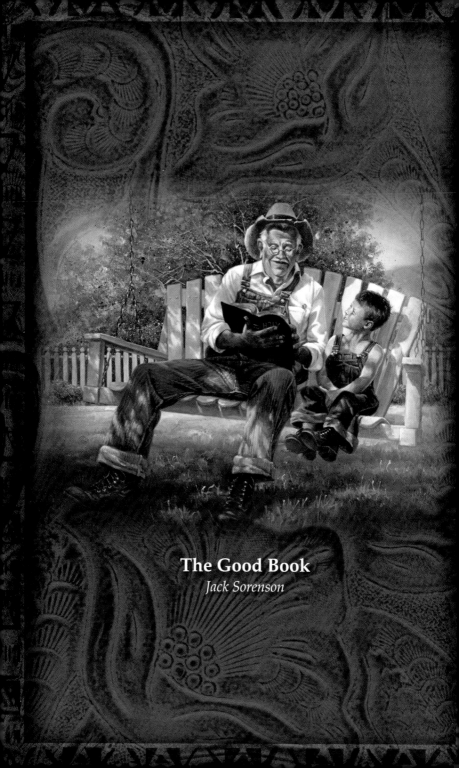

The Good Book

Jack Sorenson

Secret to Success

"This Book of the Law shall not depart from your mouth, but you shall meditate in it day and night, that you may observe to do according to all that is written in it. For then you will make your way prosperous, and then you will have good success."
Joshua 1:8

The Bible is really not God's Rule Book; it's His Success Book. In the past few decades, millions of dollars have been made and spent on success books. Most of them are good reading, and – if followed – can help one obtain "success". . . success as the world terms it. But that success is not nearly as encompassing as God's success.

Possibly one of the best definitions of God's success is realizing and obtaining the destiny that God has designed for you, as outlined in *Ephesians 2:10*, "For we are His workmanship, created in Christ Jesus for good works, which God prepared beforehand that we should walk in them."

Actually, the English word success is only used once in the entire Bible. But that use gives us all we need to know about the secret to God's success. In our lead scripture above, God told His man, Joshua, to "meditate in the word day and night" in order to have "good success."

That same key to success holds true for us today. God never changes. His ways never change. Instead of meditating and pondering on what the world has to say about the situation (i.e. television, newspapers, internet), center up on God's Word. For example, as I'm writing this, the national economic situation says we're in a deep recession, stock market continues down, unemployment rising . . . the outlook is glum. That's the time for the believer to rise and shine. Remember, the stock market -- even your employer -- is not your supply . . . God is! Take hold of His Word in your heart: "And my God shall supply all your (my) need according to His riches in glory by Christ Jesus." *(Philippians 4:19)* Then ask for, and receive by faith, the wisdom you need in your situation. *(James 1:4-6)*

Next, enter into praise and thanksgiving for your total success! And don't allow anything to the contrary to come out of your mouth.

Remember, the
stock market — even
your employer — is
not your supply . . .
God is!

Clearview
Chuck DeHaan

God-Minded

*Trust in the Lord with all your heart and lean not
on your own understanding. In all your ways
acknowledge Him and He shall direct your paths.*
Proverbs 3:5-6

My Dad, Doc Spence, had a reputation for putting the best "handle" on his horses that you could find anywhere. Dad always broke and started his colts in a hackamore, then he'd take them on to a light snaffle bit. By the time he had ridden a horse for thirty days, he'd have that youngster doing about anything he asked him with only the slightest touch on the reins.

Perhaps the best example of Dad's putting a handle on a horse was Knocky, a Quarter Horse gelding that was the Honor Roll (high point of the year) horse in the American Quarter Horse Assn. for both reining and calf roping in 1956. Dad also won the novice cutting on Knocky at the Denver National that same year.

Although I started riding about the same time I started walking, I never had the patience or ability to put a handle on a horse like Dad; it just wasn't my gift. But I never ceased to enjoy going home and getting on one of his horses to cut a few cows or maybe just ride pasture. It was such a treat to ride a horse that was so responsive and just waiting to do what you wanted him to.

A few years ago, I was warming up a horse, getting ready for a little ranch sorting, and my mind wandered back to riding with Dad, who passed away in 1990. Instantaneously, I heard that "still small voice" in my heart: *I want you to learn to be as responsive to Me as your Dad's horses were to him."*

As I mediated on those words, it occurred to me that Dad's horses were always *rider-minded.* Regardless of the task at hand, the horse never seemed to lose sight of the fact that the rider was in ultimate control. It was as if the horse had one ear on the business at hand and the other ear cocked on his rider. The passage above from Proverbs really fits in here. The Message translation puts verse six like this: "Listen for God's voice in everything you do, everywhere you go; he's the one who will keep you on track."

So, what the Word is really telling us to do is to get God-minded. But it takes some training, just like Dad's horses that were so rider-minded. For most of us, our days are so chocked full of work, family, friends, television, horses (busyness of all sorts), that we seem to have little time to be God-minded, at least other than maybe Sunday morning at church.

But that can change; it's really not that difficult. . . and just imagine the tremendous benefits of having God direct your steps and "keep you on track." For starters, think of all the dead ends, bad deals, blown turns, and missed opportunities that would be avoided! Remember, God is totally on your side, greatly desires your complete success, and is never going to lead you down the wrong path

My first step came by putting God first place every morning. . . at least first place after taking my vitamins and brewing the coffee (it's mostly decaf at this stage of the game). As soon as a full cup has run through Mr. Coffee, I take it to my easy chair and read my little devotion for the day *(God Calling),* followed by a chapter in the Word. I meditate on what I've read for ten minutes or so and just keep my ears open to anything the Lord might want to say. Sometimes I hear a word or two, but most often I'm just aware of His sweet and peaceful presence.

A little word of caution here: those results didn't come the first few times I attempted my "time with Him." The undisciplined mind has a tendency to wander, often far, far away from the things of God. You have to take hold of it, just like a green colt. (There's scripture for that in *II Corinthians 10:4-5*). But the more you practice, the better it gets. Then you'll get to the point that a team of wild mules couldn't keep you from that "quiet time in the morning."

And that sets the stage for the rest of your day in God-mindedness. You'll soon find yourself talking to Him about even the little things, asking for advice on where to go, what to say, little decisions as well as big ones.

Someone will say, "But what if I ask Him and I don't hear anything?" That's when the trust factor comes in. It's called "walking by faith" . . . and it comes by getting God-minded.

Doc Spence on Knocky, 1956.

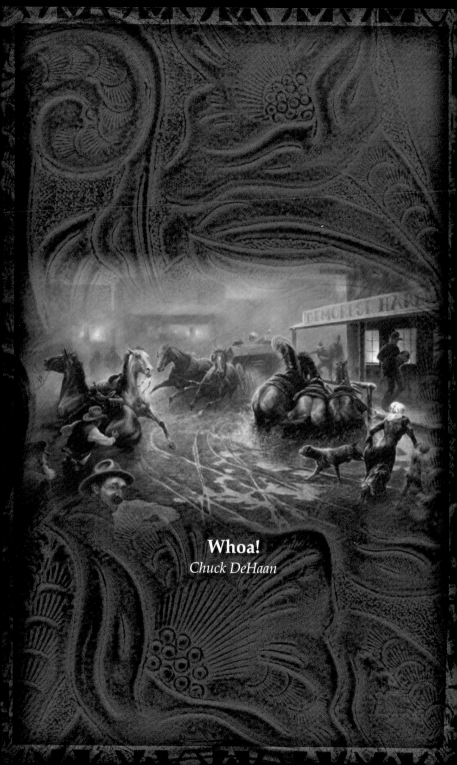

Whoa!
Chuck DeHaan

The Roadblock

For where envying and strife is, there is confusion and every evil work. But the wisdom that is from above is first pure, then peaceable, gentle, and easy to be entreated, full of mercy and good fruits, without partiality, and without hypocrisy. And the fruit of righteousness is sown in peace of them that make peace. **James 3:16-18 KJV**

All sin is costly. But there is one sin that may be more expensive to a believer than most all other shortcomings – strife.

In our scripture above, James tells us that where strife (contention and selfish ambition) exists, there is every evil work That one statement should make a Christian avoid strife like the plague.

Jesus said in *Matthew 5:23* that if you're bringing an offering to God and you remember that you're in strife with a fellow believer, stop immediately and get rid of the strife; then make the offering. The indication here is that strife is a roadblock to your being blessed from the offering.

Peter admonishes a husband to dwell in understanding and peace (free of strife) with his wife in order for there to be no roadblocks (hindrances) to their prayers *(I Peter 3:7)*.

From these and other scriptures, it's evident that the devil flourishes and feeds on strife; most likely it's his main source of nourishment. So, let's fast strife in our lives, starve the devil out, and get rid of the roadblocks to our blessings. Love the Lord with all your heart and love your neighbor as yourself . . . then strife will have no place in your life.

Down from the High Country

Jack Sorenson

The Way In

...that if you confess with your mouth the Lord Jesus and believe in your heart that God has raised Him from the dead, you will be saved. For with the heart one believes unto righteousness, and with the mouth confession is made unto salvation. For the Scripture says, "Whoever believes on Him will not be put to shame."
(Isaiah 28:16) Romans 10: 9-11

Some time ago a friend sent me a story entitled "Heaven's Entry Requirements." Seems a man died and went to heaven. Of course, St. Peter met him at the Pearly Gates and said, "Now, here's how it works . . . you need 100 points to make it in. You tell me all the good things you've done, and I'll give you a certain number of points, depending on how good it was. When you reach 100 points, you get in."

"Okay," the man said, "I was married to the same woman for 50 years and never cheated on her, not even in my heart."

"That's wonderful," said St. Peter, "that's worth three points!"

"Three points?" exclaimed the man. "Well, I attended church all my life and supported its ministries with my tithes and service."

"Terrific!" said St. Peter. "That's certainly worth a point."

"One point?!!" The man continued, "And I started a soup kitchen in my city and worked in a shelter for homeless veterans."

"Fantastic, that's good for two more points," said St. Peter.

"Two points!!!" Exasperated, the man cried out, "At this rate the only way I'll get into heaven is by the grace of God!"

"Bingo, 100 points! Come on in," said Peter with a welcoming gesture.

We've all heard a jillion of those old St. Peter -- Pearly Gates jokes, and while Peter was the Lord Jesus' right-hand man, there's not much scripture to indicate that Peter is standing guard at the Eternal Gate. Still, this is probably my favorite of all those old stories, mainly because it points out how a lot of us grew up thinking about heaven and how to get there. This, in spite of going to church and hearing that accepting Jesus Christ as my personal Savior is the *only* way to heaven . . . and in spite of that often-quoted passage above from Paul's letter to the Romans.

It's so easy in this competitive, performance-oriented culture in which we live to begin thinking that God's system operates the same as man's . . . when it's really almost opposite! Certainly God wants us to live good, moral lives, to work hard, avoid laziness, and love our neighbors. But the Bible makes it mighty clear that no amount of good works puts us in His stable. Salvation is strictly a *free gift* that cannot be earned.

Only one man ever lived this life perfectly and actually qualified for heaven by his works -- Jesus Christ, the only begotten Son of God, who came to earth as a man, lived that sinless life . . . then went to the cross where He actually *became* our sin (everybody's), then went into Hell and paid the price for all those sins – the price that you and I should have paid. It was the great exchange: our sins for His righteousness! But there's just one stipulation – you gotta believe it! That's what is pointed out in our lead scriptures from the book of Romans.

What a deal! Seems almost too simple, too easy. But somehow the culture we live in – and a great deal of religion – has made it complicated to get in. It's really not!

Raising Snow Dust
Chuck DeHaan

More Faith?

Faith is the confidence that what we hope for will actually happen; it gives us assurance about things we cannot see.
Hebrews 11:1 NLT

Most all of us have prayed at one time or another, "Lord, just give me more faith." The disciples asked Jesus to "increase our faith," when He told them how much they were supposed to walk in forgiveness *(Luke 17:3-5)*.

But Jesus said if you only had a mustard seed of faith, you could tell a mulberry tree to go jump in the lake, and it would obey you (verse 6)! Then, *Romans 12:3* ("God has dealt to each man a measure of faith"), and *2 Peter 1:1* ("like precious faith"). These scriptures confirm that we *all* have this faith.

So, it looks like we don't need *more* faith…just use what we have so that we *build* our faith. It's like muscles in the body; the biceps in our arms, for example. Everybody has them, but some develop them more than other folks do.

We were given this faith when we accepted the Lord Jesus Christ as Savior and were born again. *Colossians 2:10* says we "are complete in Him." It's right there on the inside of us – every bit of faith that we could ever need for anything. But we have to use it, develop it, put it to work by practice, practice, practice . . . by believing what God's Word says about us . . . by being "doers of the word, and not hearers only" *(James 1:22)*.

And maybe we need to start with telling a weed or two of unbelief to jump in the lake before we get to the mulberry trees.

Spring Break
Chuck DeHaan

Worry Not

"Therefore I say to you, do not worry about your life, what you will eat or what you will drink; nor about your body, what you will put on. Is not life more than food and the body more than clothing?...Which of you by worrying can add one cubit to his stature?...Consider the lilies of the field, how they grow: they neither toil nor spin; and yet I say to you that even Solomon in all his glory was not arrayed like one of these...But seek first the kingdom of God and His righteousness, and all these things shall be added to you... Therefore do not worry about tomorrow, for tomorrow will worry about its own things.
Matthew 6:25, 27, 28, 33, 34

I have a friend at the race track who, by his own admission, is a "professional worrier." His main problem can be summed up in one statement: *He dwells on past failures and is fearful of the future.* Thus far, I've not gotten him to change his thinking patterns, but I pray for him, and I know that God knows exactly how to minister to his heart.

I have empathy for my friend because I was once very much like him. One day, as I was reading what Jesus said about worry in the Sermon on the Mount, it came to me that worry does two things: changes your hair color and shortens your life. You see, worry is simply a distraction that causes anxiety, stress, and pressure – no-no's to the abundant life that Jesus has provided for us *(John 10:10).*

Actually, worry simply indicates a lack of trust in God and His unconditional love for us. Once you get it settled in your knower (heart) that God is totally on your side and is, in fact, your very best Friend, then worries fade into the sunset. Meditate on our lead passages above, *Matthew 6:25-34*, and you will discover that you are more blessed than Solomon!

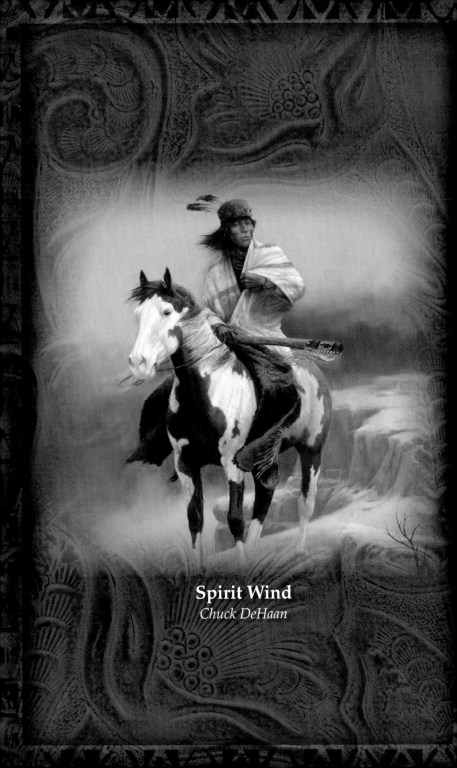

Spirit Wind
Chuck DeHaan

Perfect Peace

You will keep him in perfect peace, whose mind is stayed on You, because he trusts in You.
Isaiah 26:3

One of the greatest promises of God is outlined in the above passage in Isaiah. The Hebrew word for perfect peace is *shalom*, which implies health, happiness, well-being and total peace. In other words, everything you could hope for or need. It just doesn't get any better than that!

The key is "a mind stayed on God." Again, going back to the Hebrew language, the word for mind is a term meaning "creative imagination." It's putting God first place in your life – getting His plan and ideas as priority in every facet of your being.

"Now that's just getting a little too religious," someone will say. My answer to you is No, this is the opposite of *religion*; rather it's true *relationship*. It's the place that God intended for man (the pinnacle of His creation) to abide in Him. It's where Adam was before the fall; it's where you and I can be now through the Lord Jesus Christ.

By knowing and understanding the true nature of God, which is love (an unconditional, all-giving love), one's mind can soar through, above, and beyond any adverse circumstance or condition. This is not pretending that the circumstance does not exist; rather it's trusting in God to see you through to victory . . . that's from where comes *perfect peace*.

Eye of Freedom
Chuck DeHaan

Worthy in Him

Let us therefore come boldly to the throne of grace, that we may obtain mercy and find grace to help in time of need.
Hebrews 4:16

"Lord, I'm just an old unworthy sinner saved by grace, and I'd be satisfied with just a few crumbs from your table."

Sounds like a sweet, humble Christian prayer, but it's really just the opposite! And regretfully, it's the attitude that many of us have been reared in over the past decades. This is the prayer of a self-righteous individual (one basing their righteousness on their own works) who does not know or understand who they are in Christ Jesus and the tremendous price our Savior paid so that they are entirely worthy in God's sight.

The Apostle Paul warned the believers at Corinth who were celebrating the Lord's Supper with this kind of attitude. "Therefore, whoever eats this bread or drinks this cup of the Lord in an *unworthy manner* will be guilty of the body and blood of the Lord. But let a man examine himself, and so let him eat of the bread and drink of the cup. For he who eats and drinks in an *unworthy manner* eats and drinks judgment to himself, not discerning the Lord's body. For this reason many are weak and sick among you, and many sleep. *I Corinthians 11:27-30 (emphasis mine)*.

Too often we Christians have not received our help or healing because of this subtle "unworthy attitude of doubt" that has slipped into our hearts. Realize, instead, that Jesus has done a complete job of making us worthy . . . "Let us therefore come boldly to the throne of grace, that we may obtain mercy and find grace to help in time of need."

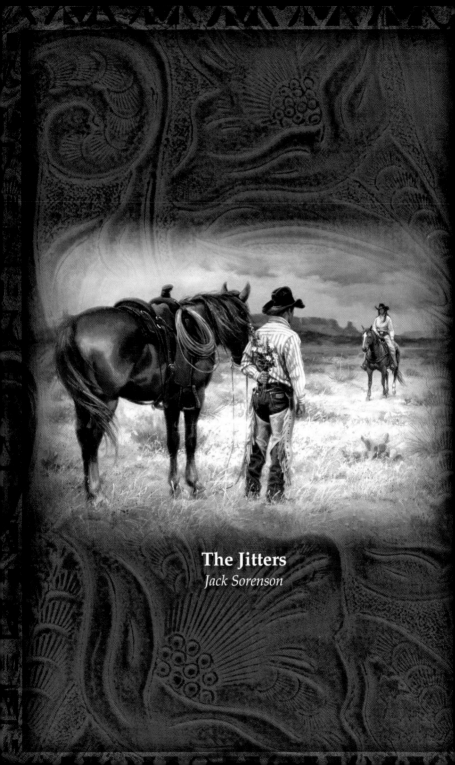

The Jitters
Jack Sorenson

Shotgun Weddings

There is no fear in love; but perfect love casts out fear, because fear involves torment. But he who fears has not been made perfect in love. **I John 4:18**

I t's an old term from years gone by when a young man was forced (at gun point, if need be) to marry a young lady when it was discovered he had taken her purity. In most cases it was "matrimony by fear," and probably seldom led to a married life of bliss… unless the reluctant couple discovered the unconditional love and forgiveness of Jesus Christ, whose *perfect love delivers from all fear.*

We (the Church) are called the bride of Christ, but I doubt He ever intended us to come on a "shotgun basis." Some of us, indeed, came in fear when we heard certain hellfire and brimstone messages that literally scared the hell out of us. We walked the aisle because we were afraid not to. Somehow, by the grace of God, some of us were actually born again. But many of us – because we weren't self-disciplined, nor had our minds renewed with God's Word – almost immediately began to backslide.

While it's true that God gives us a new heart and a new spirit when we're born again, there can still remain a "fear blockage" to having a close, intimate relationship with the One whom we think punishes people and sends them to eternal damnation for their sins.

Hell is definitely real, and there are poor souls going there every day. But God's not sending them, and He's not punishing them. It's simply their choice. The Bible makes it clear that God "desires all men to be saved and to come to the knowledge of the truth." *(I Timothy 2:4)* Again, it's our choice to receive that salvation (a free gift) and spend forever with a loving Father, or to spend eternity totally separated from Him – and that's hell!

The Bible says it's the goodness (kindness) of God that brings men to repentance. *(Romans 2:4)* But if you came to the Lord via the old shotgun, chances are you've still got some traces of fear hiding in the crevices of your heart. Take *II Timothy 1:7* and *I John 4:18* and drive out that fear, doubt, and unbelief. Then grab hold of all that fullness, peace, joy, and provision that Jesus has provided for you . . . it's free for the taking.

God desires all

men to be saved

and to come to the

knowledge of

the truth.

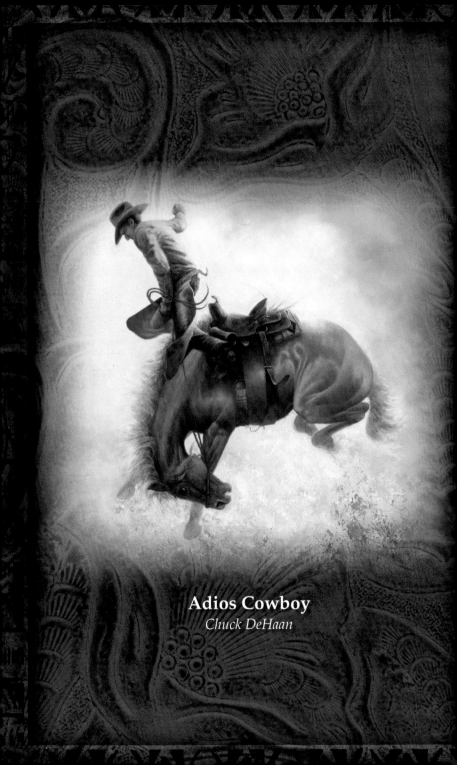

Adios Cowboy
Chuck DeHaan

The Self Life

Then God said, "Let Us make man in Our image,
according to Our likeness; let them have dominion
over the fish of the sea, over the birds of the air,
and over the cattle, over all the earth and over
every creeping thing that creeps on the earth."
Genesis 1:26

Who's running this show?

Obviously, we are – you and I, descendents of the first man, Adam, whom God created in His image and gave dominion (rule, control) over the earth.

So, how's it working out for us?

Overall, not too spiffy! Look around the world . . . it's full of greed, violence, hunger, wars, power struggles, poverty, disease, addictions, and fear. We know that all began when Adam started doing his own thing (at the devil's suggestion) rather than walk in the wisdom, fellowship, and intimate love of the Father.

The first man opted for the self life. And for the most part, everyone else followed suit for the next few thousand years.

Then God sent His Son, Jesus the Christ, to walk as a man like all those before Him, with the same self will and freedoms to choose. Unlike the first Adam, however, this One didn't fall for the devil's wily schemes. Instead, He chose to stay tight with the Father, doing only what He saw the Father do and speaking only what He heard the Father speak *(John 14:10).* Jesus nixed the self life.

Then this perfect "son of man" went to the cross and actually became all the sins of the world, from the first Adam to the last human being who will ever live on the earth as we know it today. For those of us who have accepted and believed in that substitutional sacrifice of Jesus, we have yet another option: To keep calling all the shots, or to die to the self life and move back into that prosperous, abundant garden paradise that was God's plan from the beginning.

But it's our choice. We can "put God first place in everything we do and let Him direct our steps" *(Proverbs 3:6 NLT),* or we can keep running the show. Evidence indicates God's better at it!

Then this perfect
"son of man" went
to the cross and
actually became all
the sins of the world.

72 Degrees in Amarillo, Yesterday
Chuck DeHaan

The Want-to to Want To

Likewise the Spirit also helps in our weaknesses.
For we do not know what we should pray for as we
ought, but the Spirit Himself makes intercession for
us with groanings which cannot be uttered.
Romans 8:26

There are times when I feel about as spiritual as
a dishrag, a wet, smelly dishrag at that! It's
usually the times when I procrastinate on something
I know I should be doing, but don't. Maybe even
something the Lord has instructed me to do or simply
to believe Him for, but don't.

These are the times when I have to call on my hedge
prayer. It's pretty simple: "Lord, give me the want-to
to want to."

That may sound foolish to you, but it's not to me,
because it works. You see, I know that a battle is
going on between my spirit and my soul. My spirit is
the real me, that God-like part of me that is born again
and is therefore perfect. My soul – basically my mind,
will and emotions – is still in the process of "being
saved," but it ain't there yet.

Hence, there's this tug of war going on inside me.
I think this is part of what the Apostle Paul was
referring to in the seventh chapter of Romans: "For
I know that in me (that is, in my flesh) nothing good

dwells; for to will is present with me, but how to perform what is good I do not find. For the good that I will to do, I do not do; but the evil I will not to do, that I practice. Now if I do what I will not to do, it is no longer I who do it, but sin that dwells in me. I find then a law, that evil is present with me, the one who wills to do good. For I delight in the law of God according to the inward man. But I see another law in my members, warring against the law of my mind, and bringing me into captivity to the law of sin which is in my members." *(Romans 7: 18-23)*

I'm convinced that my little hedge prayer is actually my spirit-man calling out to my sleepy conscience saying, "I'm here and I'm available; just give me a shot and we'll get this ball rolling."

The great thing about this prayer is that it takes less than a mustard seed of faith to work. And it's a wonderful testimony to the Lord, who promised that He *would never leave us nor forsake us* . . . regardless of our feelings, performance, or dishrag odor. In fact, He had to give me the want-to to want to write this.

He will never
leave us nor
forsake us.

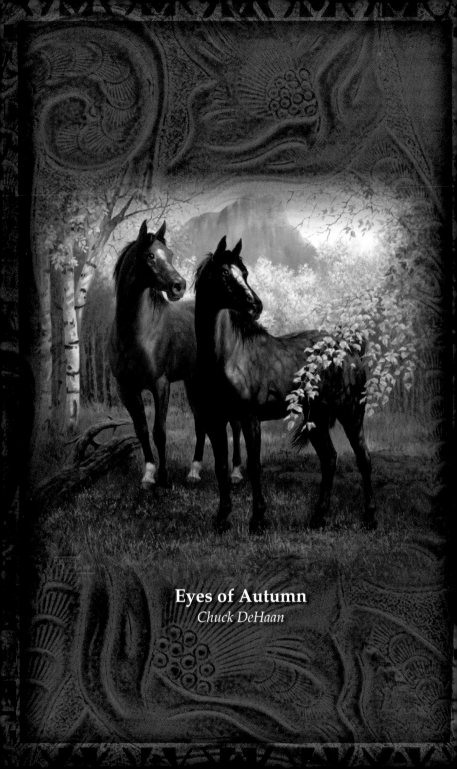

Eyes of Autumn
Chuck DeHaan

It Is Well

Therefore take up the whole armor of God, that you may be able to withstand in the evil day, and having done all, to stand. **Ephesians 6:13**

One of the great lessons on faith in the Old Testament is found in the fourth chapter of II Kings, the story of the Shunammite woman.

After having received a "miracle son" from God as a reward for her kindness to the prophet Elisha, the Shunammite woman's son (a few years later) died in her arms, evidently the victim of a heat stroke.

Yet, this woman refused to accept defeat . . . and she did not allow any negative words to come from her mouth. When asked by her husband why she was requesting a donkey and a young man as a driver to get her to Elisha, the Shunammite's only answer was "it is well!"

She then proceeded full speed via burro to Elisha's residence at Mount Carmel, about a 15-mile trip. On arrival, the woman's only comment to Gehazi, Elisha's servant, was again "it is well."

Elisha finally got the message and proceeded to the Shunammite's home, where -- after prayer and instructions from God -- he raised the boy from the dead and presented him to his mother.

Lesson: Just because we receive a great blessing from God doesn't keep the world, circumstances, or the devil from trying to steal that blessing from us. When that happens, refuse to be negative. Go to God and His Word for the solution. Then, having done all, stand until the answer comes. And remember, *it is well*.

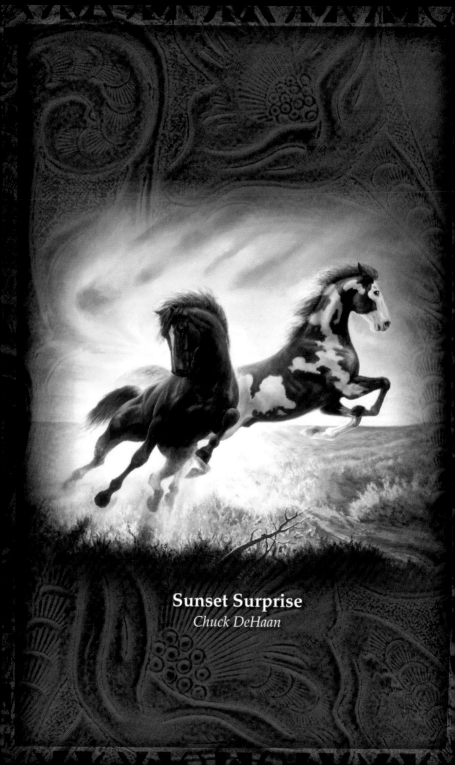

Sunset Surprise
Chuck DeHaan

Bombarding the Gates

*"Therefore I say to you, whatever things you ask
when you pray, believe that you receive them, and
you will have them."*
Mark 11:24

I've said it, you've probably said it, and we've heard it umpteen times in Christian circles over the years: "We've got to bombard the gates of heaven with our prayers . . ."

Actually, this is an unscriptural statement; one that does not reflect the true nature of our heavenly Father. In fact, it's almost a slap in the face of Jesus because it suggests that He didn't get a complete job done at the cross!

"So, Chaplain, are you saying that we don't need to pray so much?" someone will ask.

Of course not. But I am saying we need to do the right kind of praying – praying in faith.

Perhaps the first step for some of us is to get out of the frame of mind that prayer is trying to change God's mind or talk Him into something (which is indicated by "bombarding the gates").

Everything that you or I could ever need was provided through the death, burial and resurrection of the Lord Jesus . . . be it wisdom, healing, protection, peace, or provision. We don't need to talk Father God into giving it to us; we simply have to believe in our hearts and receive it.

Observe what Jesus Himself tells us in the scripture above from Mark's gospel. There's just nothing here that indicates a need for bombardment, begging, or pleading of any type. The only thing needing bombardment is the doubt or unbelief that can rise up in our hearts and keep us from receiving what our Savior has already provided.

Little Boys Dream the Biggest Dreams
Tim Cox

The Dreamer

Delight yourself also in the Lord, and He shall give you the desires of your heart. Psalms 37:4

I n the thirty-seventh chapter of Genesis, we find Joseph, the teenage son of Jacob, having a couple of dreams that gave him hope of great blessings, including him becoming the head of all his family. However, over the next few years, Joseph went from one calamity to another. He'd jump out of the frying pan, only to end up in the fire! Circumstances continually said to him, "Forget it, boy; those dreams you had were nothing more than glorified nightmares. You're never going to amount to anything."

But Joseph refused to give up hope. He knew that his dreams were from God, and He trusted that God would not let him down. Sure enough, in the midst of dire circumstances, Joseph – in one 24-hour period – went from being a destitute prisoner in a smelly dungeon to the most powerful man in Egypt, second only to Pharaoh the King. And his dreams became a living reality.

I'm convinced that God puts a dream in the heart of every one of His children. It could be a dream to be a great leader, or simply a dream to lead a quiet, peaceful life and be a blessing to those around you. It could be a dream to have a family, or to come out of poverty or some debilitating sickness or disease.

Many have never realized that God not only puts those dreams (desires) in our hearts, but that He truly wants to bring them to fruition. However, He needs our cooperation of faith and hope to fulfill those dreams . . . "He is a rewarder of those who diligently seek him." *(Hebrews 11:6)*

Don't let contrary circumstances rob you of your dreams. Take hold of God's Word in your heart . . . and don't let go! And don't quit dreaming.

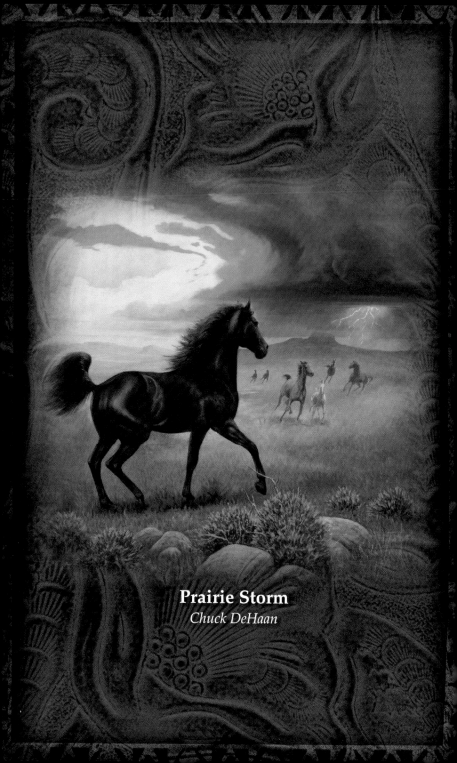

Prairie Storm
Chuck DeHaan

The Still Small Voice

And behold, the LORD passed by, and a great and strong wind tore into the mountains and broke the rocks in pieces before the LORD , but the LORD was not in the wind; and after the wind an earthquake, but the LORD was not in the earthquake; and after the earthquake a fire, but the LORD was not in the fire; and after the fire a still small voice.
1 Kings 19:11, 12

One of the interesting aspects of our scriptures here is that God was not the author, nor was He involved in the catastrophic winds, earthquake, or fire. And yet, so often we credit the LORD with huge *natural* disasters. Even many of our insurance policies excuse themselves from covering these "acts of God." But these acts do not line up with the Bible's definition of our heavenly Father, which is love *(1 John 4:16)*, an unconditional love that never changes. And love never destroys people or property.

Perhaps the primary message from these scriptures is how God so often speaks to us – *a still small voice*, as opposed to a booming catastrophe. But to hear the voice, we usually have to get still in our soul – our mind, will, and emotions.

"Slow down and listen," is how the Holy Spirit put it to me several years ago. It's advice I have to remind myself of almost daily. A tremendous help in hearing His voice came by diligently setting aside a *quiet time* the first thing each morning. That sets the stage for hearing throughout the day.

I was amazed – and I think you will be, too – at how much the LORD desires to converse with each of His children.

Yep, there He is again: "Can you hear Me now?"

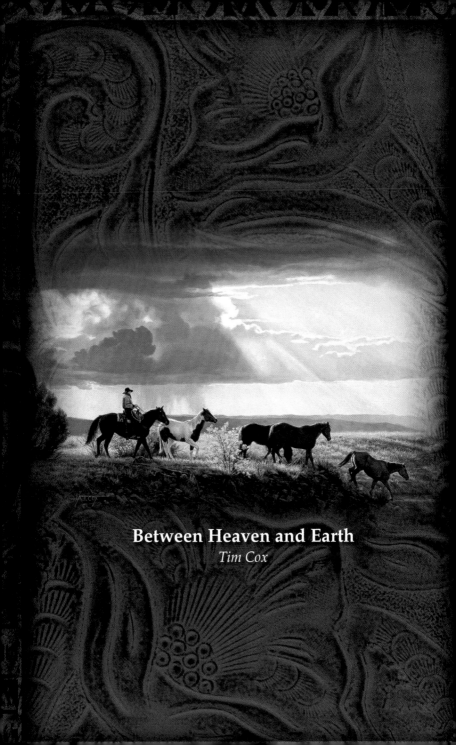

Between Heaven and Earth
Tim Cox

The Big Fallacy

For by grace you have been saved through faith, and that not of yourselves; it is the gift of God, not of works, lest anyone should boast.
Ephesians 2:8,9

Had a conversation recently in a shedrow, and the fellow I was talking with brought up the subject of heaven. A little later in our talk I asked him, "So, how do you think you'll get to heaven?" His answer fell in line with what I've heard many times over the years: "By believing in God and basically being a good person." In my mind I could hear that big buzzer going off that you hear on some TV quiz show when a wrong answer is given.

"Now I've not been a preacher or a chaplain like you," my shedrow friend continued, "but I've never killed or hurt anyone, and I think I do a fairly good job of walking the straight and narrow." He then admitted that he really felt he had more pluses than minuses in that "big chart book" God was keeping.

I understood exactly where he was coming from; in fact, I held those same misconceptions for the first 33-plus years of my life, although I was probably a lot less confident than my friend that my chart book was looking that good. Still, I didn't come down on him; I simply shared a few scriptures that I wanted him to think about.

First off, in the second chapter of James, the writer says, "You believe there is one God. You do well. Even the demons believe – and tremble! *(James 2:19)* In other words, just believing there is a God doesn't count for much.

Now, let's go on to my friend's other reasoning for being heaven-bound – "a fairly good job of walking the straight and narrow." But our lead scripture above points out that salvation is strictly a gift and has nothing to do with our wonderful works. Keeping the rules and doing good stuff is commendable; something we should all do . . . but that won't get us through the pearly gates.

So, what's the answer; how do you get in? In a nutshell, *Romans 10:9-10* has it: "that if you confess with your mouth the Lord Jesus and believe in your heart that God has raised Him from the dead, you will be saved. For with the heart one believes unto righteousness, and with the mouth confession is made unto salvation."

It's all about Jesus, the only one who was actually perfect enough to make it to heaven on His own. Instead, He went to the cross, actually became our sin, then went into hell and paid the price that we should have paid for all our shortcomings. Because of Jesus Christ, salvation is truly a *gift* of God. To think it can be earned is *the big fallacy.*

For with the heart
one believes unto
righteousness, and
with the mouth
confession is made
unto salvation.

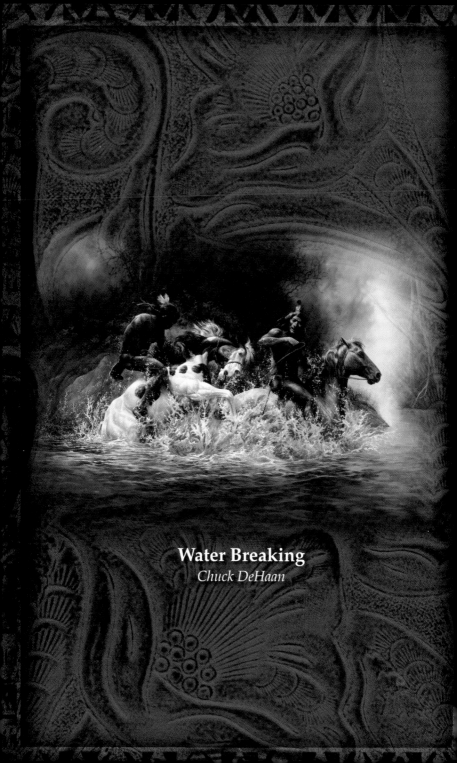

Water Breaking
Chuck DeHaan

The Limiting Factor

*Now He did not do many mighty works there
because of their unbelief.*
Matthew 13:58

In the thirteenth chapter of Matthew, we find Jesus
doing wonderful miracles and healing multitudes
by the Sea of Galilee. Then, after a tremendous
teaching on the parables, Jesus departed and went
over to his hometown of Nazareth, less than 20 miles
away. There He continued His great teaching in the
local synagogue.

However, Jesus was met with resistance by the people
in Nazareth. They simply couldn't accept the fact that
this carpenter's son – this hometown boy they had
seen grow up there in years past – could teach and do
such wonderful feats.

The only limiting factor to God doing wonderful
things in their midst and in their very lives was their
unbelief – their refusal to accept what God truly had
for them.

How often do you and I limit God in doing mighty
works in our lives? Jesus said "all things are possible
to him who believes." *(Mark 9:23)* So, fight unbelief
with every ounce of Word in you. Get rid of the
limiting factor.

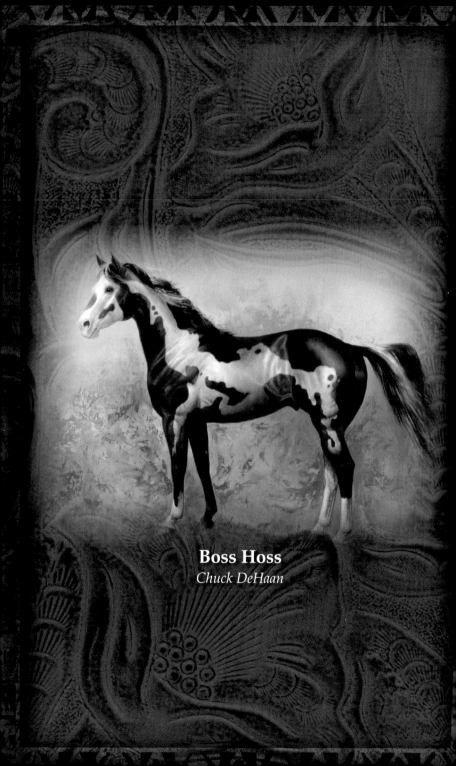

Boss Hoss
Chuck DeHaan

Bloom Where You're Planted

And the Syrians had gone out on raids, and had
brought back captive a young girl from the land
of Israel. She waited on Naaman's wife.
2 Kings 5:2

The young lady in our scripture above could have
been bitter about being taken captive and made
a slave. Instead, she chose to share God's healing
power that worked through the prophet in Israel.
Consequently, not only was Naaman, the commander
of the Syrian army, saved and healed of leprosy, but
there were most likely many others who came to
know and believe in the God of Israel.

This little slave girl, regardless of her circumstances,
was a witness for the Lord. She chose to bloom where
she was planted. We need to do the same. Regardless
of where we are, we need to share the love of God
with those around us. You might well be God's rose in
a weed patch.

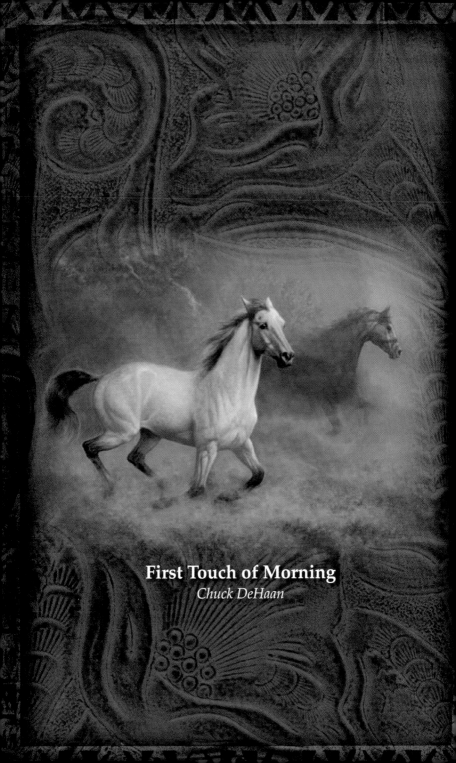

First Touch of Morning
Chuck DeHaan

Joy

But the fruit of the Spirit is love, joy, peace,
longsuffering, kindness, goodness, faithfulness,
gentleness, self-control. Against such there is no law.
Galatians 5:22, 23

Have you noticed that the second fruit which Paul lists in those nine beautiful fruit of the Spirit is JOY? Meditating on that recently, I was impressed by the Lord that if I would make *love* (the first fruit and obviously the most important) and *joy* the priorities in my life, then the remaining seven fruit would follow without effort – almost automatically.

Joy is something that goes much deeper than happiness. You can be happy over a birthday present or in shooting a par round of golf (downright hilarity for me!). But true *joy* comes from deep within your being – the *joy* of having a personal, intimate relationship with your Creator . . . the *joy* of knowing that you'll never be judged by Him for the shortcomings in your life . . . the joy of knowing in your heart that you are loved unconditionally. And that's how "the joy of the Lord (becomes) our strength." *(Nehemiah 8:10b)*

Laughter is a side effect of joy. In fact, in the last several years, scientific research has discovered that laughing is one of the healthiest things you can do. Among the many attributes of laughter, it releases endorphins in your brain that promote healing in your body. Interestingly, He who designed us that way also said, "A merry heart does good like medicine." *(Proverbs 17:22)*

Most all of my life, I've been a jokester. I really enjoy a good joke, and I equally enjoy making others laugh. I truly think it was a gift from God; however, regretfully, in the first 33-plus years of my life a great deal of my humor and jokes were at someone else's expense . . . and the humor did little to glorify the Lord.

Then, after coming into fellowship with the Lord and getting to know Him, I found out that Jesus has the greatest sense of humor of any man. The best laughs I've ever experienced have been in my "quiet times" with the Lord – those times when all the distractions of the world are *tuned-out* and I'm *tuned-in* to Him. I can't recall the last time I started out my day without something Jesus gave me to smile about. I can attest to what David said in *Psalm 16:11* . . . "In Your presence is fullness of joy."

Going back to that fifth chapter of Galatians where Paul was teaching on the fruit of the Spirit, early in that section of his letter, the Apostle admonished the Christians in Galatia about forfeiting the liberty they had in Christ. They were getting themselves "entangled again with a yoke of bondage" – trying to live by the old law, which is never joyful. Paul made the statement, "A little leaven leavens the whole loaf" (verse 9). As I was reading that, the Lord dropped a little nugget on me: *"And a little levity lightens the whole load!"*

That's the way to fly – love and laughter!

True joy comes
from deep within
your being — the joy
of having a personal,
intimate relationship
with your Creator.

Freedom
Chuck DeHaan

The Name

"And these signs shall follow those who believe: In My name they will cast out demons; they will speak with new tongues; they will take up serpents; and if they drink anything deadly, it will by no means hurt them; they will lay hands on the sick, and they will recover."

Mark 16:17, 18

When God created man, He gave him dominion and instructions to rule and subdue the earth and everything in it. *(Genesis 1:26, 28)* We know, of course, that the first man, Adam, blew the deal and actually committed high treason by obeying Satan and handing his (Adam's) authority over to the devil.

But when Jesus Christ went to the cross, stood in for us, and then defeated the devil and all his cohorts *(Colossians 2:13-15)*, He got back that dominion and authority that Adam had forfeited in the garden. In our scripture above, Jesus is telling us that we have the "power of attorney" over the devil and all his junk.

Notice He did not say these signs shall follow chaplains, preachers, ministers or priests . . . rather, simply *those who believe;* those who are born again and will speak *The Name* in faith. It's yours to use.

Sudden Death

Russell Houston

Nobody Ever Went to Hell for Drinkin'

*And He [that same Jesus Himself] is the propitiation
(the atoning sacrifice) for our sins, and not for ours
alone but also for [the sins of] the whole world.*
I John 2:2 AMP

Our title here might be contrary to what you think or what your religion has taught you…but it's truth. The only thing that keeps anyone out of heaven (and sends them to that other place) is the failure or refusal to accept the fact that Jesus Christ paid the price for their sins.

To say that a man or woman went to hell for being an alcoholic, or a drug addict, or an adulterer, even a murderer . . . is to say that Jesus did an incomplete job when He went to the cross. The Bible says that Jesus actually *became* our sin (all the sins that have been, or ever will be, committed in this earth). Then He went into hell Himself and suffered an incomprehensible punishment for all those sins, punishment that was due us. And through this big exchange, Jesus satisfied the wrath of God against mankind; we were reconciled to Him *(Romans 5:10)*. Reconcile means to change, exchange, reestablish, restore relationships, make things right and remove an enmity. That's exactly what Jesus Christ accomplished for you and me.

So, is this a blank check to be a sot, a druggie, an adulterer, etc., and wallow in all that sin that's so much "fun for a season?" Of course not! Simply say "no" to that which will bring you hell on this earth!

The reason God wants us to stay out of sin is because it hurts us and those around us . . . and God doesn't want us hurting. He wants us happy, whole, blessed and prospering at all levels. God is not the author of hurt – sin is. So, steer clear of it.

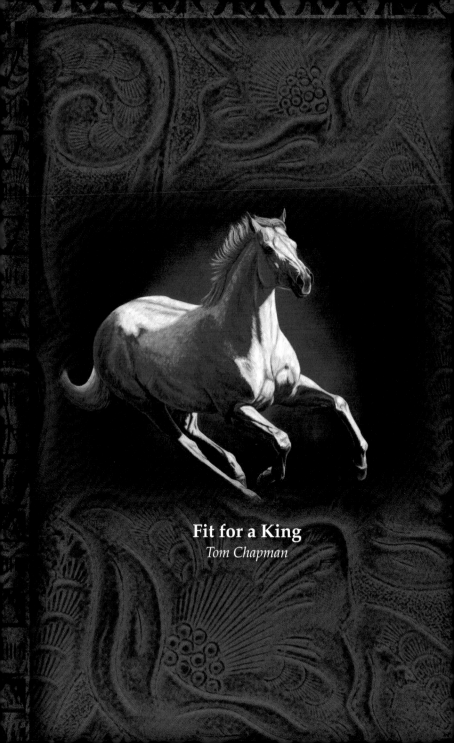

Fit for a King
Tom Chapman

Fly With Me

There is no fear in love; but perfect love casts out fear,
because fear involves torment. But he who fears has
not been made perfect in love. **I John 4:18**

Shortly after graduating from college – long years
ago – I took a job that required me to travel
about three weekends of each month. Over the next
two years I put in 50-75,000 miles a year in air travel.
I don't recall having any fear of flying, although I
did get nauseous a couple of times on some bumpy
"puddle-hopper" flights through the mountains.

A number of years later, after coming to the Lord, I
was listening to tent evangelist R. W. Shambach on
his radio program tell of a near mid-flight disaster
that was narrowly avoided in a plane he was in
outside Chicago. When asked if that made him
"afraid to fly," Brother Shambach readily replied,
"Absolutely not; in fact, if you want to fly on a safe
airplane, just fly with me!"

That statement exploded on the inside of me. I
claimed it for myself, because I knew where Brother
Shambach was coming from. He had hold of the
love of God, the love that "casts out fear." Over the
years I've made that same statement to a number of
people . . . "come fly with me if you want to get on a
guaranteed safe airplane."

"But, Chaplain," some say, "you're just flat cocky

and presumptuous."

Not really. I just believe God's Word and His love for me. In fact, I'll take it a step further: If Jesus tarries, I refuse to leave this life via sickness, disease *or* accident. I refuse to allow fear to rob me of the destiny God has for me in this world.

I know what Jesus Christ did for me through his death, burial, and resurrection, and I – for one – am taking advantage of it. But guess what? God doesn't love me one iota more than He loves you or any other individual! I'm totally convinced that He deeply desires each of His children to *live in faith* and experience this tremendous love He has for us that drives out all fear.

Listen, you can hear Him saying now, "Child, come fly with me!"

I refuse to allow
fear to rob me of the
destiny God has for
me in this world.

Two Horses
Chuck DeHaan

God's Will

Beloved, I pray that you may prosper in every way and [that your body] may keep well, even as [I know] your soul keeps well and prospers. **3 John 2 AMP**

This is one of the most encompassing scriptures in the New Testament concerning God's will for our lives. When the Apostle John penned these words under the unction and direction of the Holy Spirit, he was giving us great revelation of the unconditional love and perfect will of the Father for *all* His children . . . to live in prosperity of health, wealth, and peace of mind.

However, because this message has been resisted (even preached against) in the body of Christ, far too few of us have walked in that perfect will. We've either been double-minded *(James 1:6-8)*, fearful, or just downright ignorant of what God has provided for us through the death, burial and resurrection of our Lord Jesus Christ.

But when one gets it settled in his or her heart about this perfect will of God, faith begins to rise; then comes the healing, the prosperity, the peace that passes understanding. And the Father is pleased to see His kids doing His will.

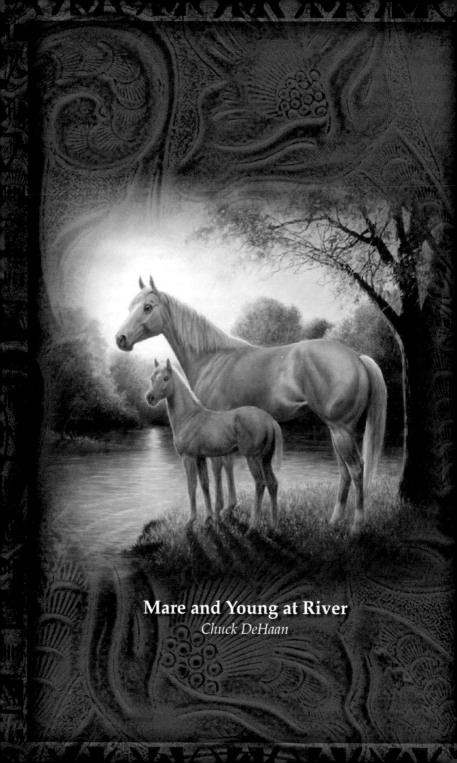

Mare and Young at River
Chuck DeHaan

You've Already Got It

"And he said to him, 'Son, you are always with me, and all that I have is yours.'" **Luke 15:31**

One of the greatest revelations that a new believer – and for some older ones, too – can get is that prayer is *not* trying to talk God into something!

You don't need to convince God to give or do something for you . . . He's already done it! And the answer to your prayer is residing right there on the inside of you. You simply need to get the right attitude in your heart to bring the answer into manifestation. Look closely at the following scriptures:

"For in Him dwells all the fullness of the Godhead bodily; and you are complete in Him, who is the head of all principality and power." *(Colossians 2:9-10)*

"Furthermore, because we are united with Christ, we have received an inheritance from God, for he chose us in advance, and he makes everything work out according to his plan." *(Ephesians 1:11 NLT)*

"'Son, you are always with me, and all that I have is yours.'" *(Luke 15:31)*

"For by grace you have been saved (set free from sin, healed, delivered from oppression, prospered) through faith, and that not of yourselves; it is a gift of God." *(Ephesians 2:8; parenthesis mine)*

"For assuredly, I say to you, whoever says to this mountain, 'Be removed and be cast into the sea,' and does not doubt in his heart, but believes that those things he says will be done, he will have whatever he says. Therefore I say to you, whatever things you ask when you pray, believe that you receive them, and you will have them." *(Mark 11:23-24)*

Meditate these scriptures – get them settled in your heart – and your prayer life concerning your personal needs or desires will change from *asking* Him to *thanking* Him that you already have it. The manifestation has to follow.

You don't need to
convince God to give
or do something for
you . . . He's already
done it!

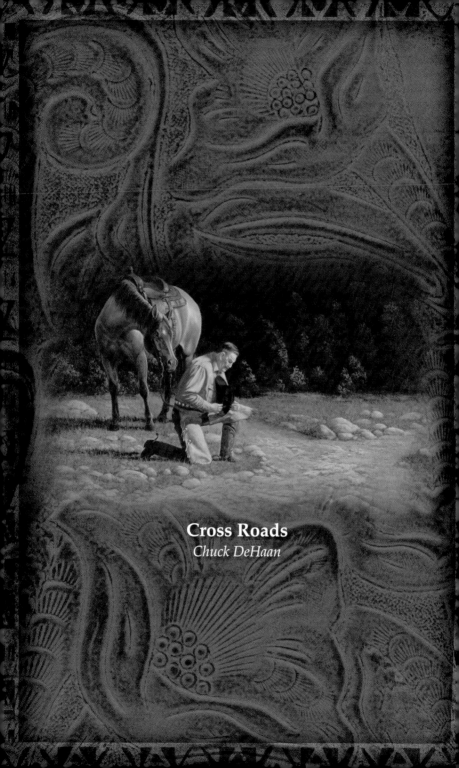

Cross Roads
Chuck DeHaan

Choose Life

". . . I have set before you life and death, blessing and cursing; therefore choose life, that both you and your descendants may live;" **Deuteronomy 30:19**

God always leaves every decision to us. That's how perfect love (the love of God) operates. It never manipulates, never controls, never forces. God suggests, He woos, He leads, He impresses, He offers direction . . . yet, the final decision is always ours.

Love says, "I'll show you the best way to go, but because I love you unconditionally, you make the choice." And even when we refuse His way, blow the turn, and end up in pain, defeat, or turmoil, He still loves us and forgives us. That's His mercy, which endures forever. It was made available for us through the death, burial, and resurrection of the Lord Jesus Christ. But it's still our choice to receive and experience it.

Under the Old Covenant, before Jesus came on the scene as a man, God spoke to the Israelites through Moses in the scripture above. God not only gave them a choice, He advised them on which choice to make. Regretfully, most all of that generation of the Jewish nation did not take God's advice. That generation died in the desert without experiencing the Promised Land, except for two men – Joshua and Caleb. These two chose to believe God and obey Him. They chose life. Consequently, they inherited and took possession of the land and all that God had promised.

Even after we have received Jesus as our Savior, we have daily choices to follow Him, or do our own thing. Jesus said, "I am the Way, the Truth, and the Life . . ." *(John 14:6)* So, choose life.

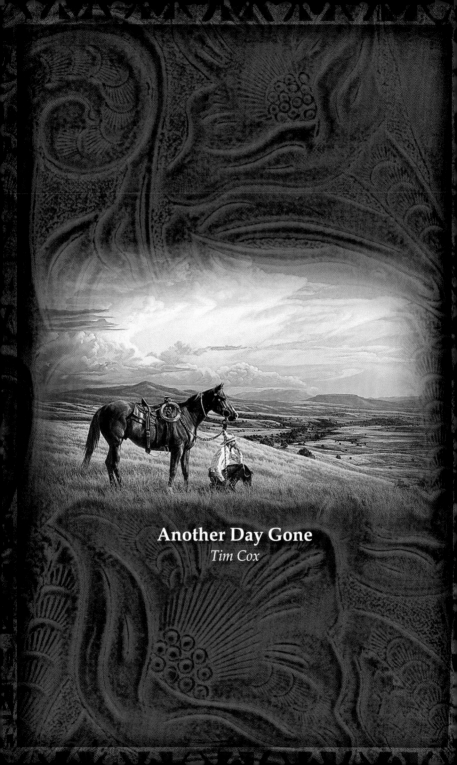

Another Day Gone
Tim Cox

The Thought Life

For as he (a man) thinks in his heart, so is he.
Proverbs 23:7

What do you spend most of your time thinking about?

The scripture above indicates that I can actually *think* my way into success, *think* my way into joy, think my way into prosperity, *think* my way into health, etc.

"So, Chaplain, you must be one of those 'positive-thinking, meditation-type gurus?'" Yep. Sure am, because it's very scriptural!

The Apostle Paul said "Finally, brethren, whatever things are true, whatever things are noble, whatever things are just, whatever things are pure, whatever things are lovely, whatever things are of good report, if there is any virtue and if there is anything praiseworthy – *meditate* on these things." *(Philippians 4:8, emphasis mine)*

It's pretty difficult to read the New Testament with an open mind (free from religious tradition) and not see that God wants us to have a high quality of life. For example, *3 John 2* says "Beloved, I pray that you may prosper in all things and be in health, just as your soul prospers." John, who was one of Jesus' closest disciples, wrote those words under the unction of the Holy Spirit, and you can rest assured that John only prayed the perfect will of God. That certainly sounds like God wants you and me to have a high quality of life!

When you start *thinking* this way, you automatically find yourself *doing* the actions and works that will cause these positive things in your life to come into manifestation. Some folks might refer to this as "putting feet to your faith."

But thinking in this mode will require a discipline in your life – a discipline of setting aside most of the TV you watch, most of your newspaper reading, even a setting aside of relationships that lead your thinking astray. You'll also need to set aside daydreaming on things of the world that are contrary to God's Word.

Know that change is available to you and will come as you begin thinking on God's Word. And remember, God is a positive thinker when it comes to thoughts about you.

God wants you
and me to have
a high quality
of life!

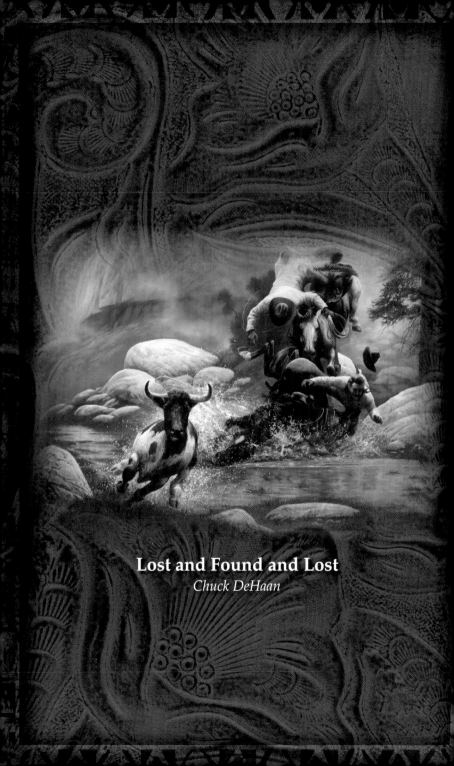

Lost and Found and Lost
Chuck DeHaan

God's Not Moody

Jesus Christ is the same yesterday, today, and forever.
Hebrews 13:8

D riving to the track one morning, it suddenly hit me how thankful I was that my heavenly Father is not moody. Instead, He's very constant – "He changes not." *(Psalm 15:4)* How comforting it is to know that God doesn't have down days or blue Mondays or TGIF's when He sighs and says, "Sure glad the weekend's here; I was needing a break."

What prompted this thankfulness in me was a compromising circumstance that occurred the day before, coupled with a "negative" dream that night. These two episodes would normally have ushered in considerable moodiness, even some depression. I knew I had not handled the situation the previous day the way I should . . . that I had really "got in the flesh" and not looked to the Holy Spirit for wisdom and strength. A voice said, "You sure let God down yesterday; can you really expect Him to come through now on that big deal you're believing Him for?"

I recognized "the accuser of the brethren" immediately, and that's when it hit me that I could be so thankful for my Father's unchangeableness. There was a time, some years back, when I would have allowed that wrong kind of thinking to lead me into a negative outlook and depression that could have lasted for several hours, even days. But the more time I spent in His Word and in quality alone-time with Him, the more I came to realize His true nature of unconditional love that had nothing whatsoever to do with my performance. Jesus had already paid the price for my mistakes, even my wrong attitudes. I just needed to get rid of that "stinking thinking" that would allow any negativism in my being.

After all, "if God is for us, who can be against us?" *(Romans 8:31)* . . . and how wonderful it is that He's not moody!

Quiet Time
Tim Cox

A Place in His Heart

God decided in advance to adopt us into his own family by bringing us to himself through Jesus Christ. This is what he wanted to do, and it gave him great pleasure. **Ephesians 1:5 NLT**

I had never heard the particular phrase before, and it certainly was not a part of my brief notes on "God's Love" which I was using in that Sunday track chapel service several years back; however, I suddenly heard myself exclaim, "There's a place in the heart of God that only you can satisfy!"

I knew immediately that those words had come from the Holy Spirit . . . they probably had more impact on me than anyone in the congregation that morning. As I meditated on the statement later, I began to realize more fully that each of us brings great pleasure to Father God like nothing else He has ever created. It speaks of the vastness of God's love; at the same time of the individuality of that love and the unique place that each of us has with Him.

This revelation has been great incentive for me to pursue a deeper relationship with my heavenly Father, to better understand His nature of love. I pray it will for you, too.

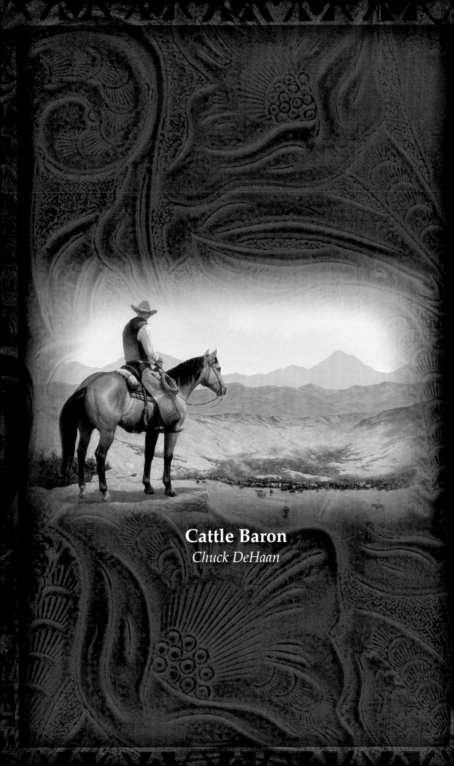

Cattle Baron
Chuck DeHaan

The Whole Enchilada

And you are complete in Him, who is the head of all principality and power. **Colossians 2:10**

In Texas we have a saying, "the whole enchilada," which refers to "a complete package," or "the whole deal," or "nothing missing."

Do you realize that when Jesus Christ went to the cross, He got "the whole enchilada" for you and me? That's right, there was nothing left out of our needs for this life – or the one hereafter – because of the death, burial and resurrection of the Lord Jesus Christ. It was a package deal that included our peace, our provision, our health, our deliverance, our protection, and our prosperity in every area, as well as our ticket to eternal life with our heavenly Father. In our scripture above, the Apostle Paul confirms that we are *complete in Him.*

This was all prophesied by Isaiah hundreds of years before Jesus came to earth as a man (*Isaiah 53:4-6*, as well as in many verses of the Psalms and Proverbs). Now, to enjoy and experience the complete package in this life, you must *believe it in your heart.*

That fifty-third chapter of Isaiah begins with "Who has believed our report?" This indicates that the only thing separating you and me from the Lord's complete provision is doubt and unbelief. Search your heart today, and let God's Word drive out any doubt that would deprive you of *the whole enchilada!*

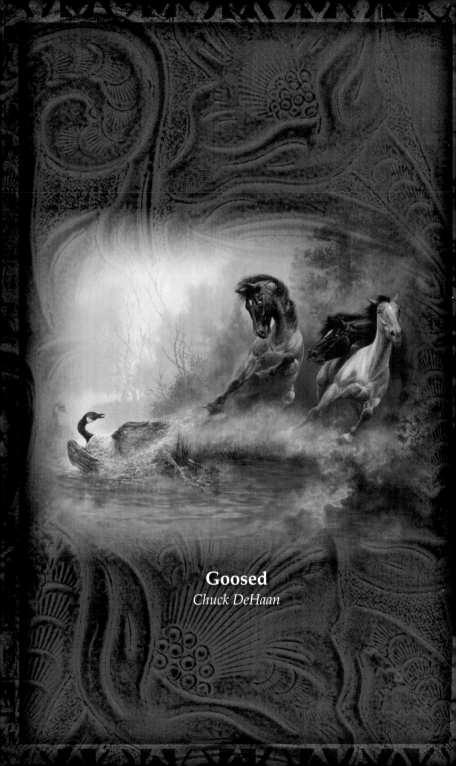

Goosed

Chuck DeHaan

Love vs. Fear

We love Him, because He first loved us. **John 4:19**

W hat's the opposite of love?

Most of us would immediately answer "hate." But that's not the answer the Bible gives. It's best exact opposite for love is *fear*. According to *I John 4:18*, "Perfect love casts out fear." Here's how the Amplified Bible says it: "There is no fear in love [dread does not exist], but full-grown (complete, perfect) love turns fear out of doors and expels every trace of terror! For fear brings with it the thought of punishment, and [so] he who is afraid has not reached the full maturity of love [is not yet grown into love's complete perfection]."

For the first 33-plus years of my life (I'm now an experienced septuagenarian), I lived in a fear of punishment from God. Even after finding out that Jesus had taken the punishment for my sins, I still had apprehensions of a "final judgment" of my shortcomings . . . and maybe some spiritual trips to the Lord's woodshed when I really blew a turn.

But then, as I began to comprehend the unconditional love of God and the *completeness* of Jesus' work at Calvary, those fears and doubts just melted away. And, instead of a spanking from the Lord when I missed the mark, He'd simply pick me up, dust me off and say, "It's okay, son; I paid for that, too . . . now let's go win this next one."

Now that's a Savior you can really fall in love with. His perfect love has wiped out all my fears. "We love Him, because He first loved us."

Moonlight
Chuck DeHaan

The Plan

For I know the thoughts that I think toward you, says the LORD, thoughts of peace and not of evil, to give you a future and a hope. **Jeremiah 29: 11**

Even before the foundations of the world were laid, God not only had you in mind, but He had a wonderful plan for your life, a plan "of peace and not of evil." Many of us have difficulty getting our minds wrapped around this fact, especially when we have experienced great failure, heartache, and lack in our lives or witnessed it in the lives around us. "What happened to The Plan?" you ask.

First off, one must understand that God has not failed . . . He never fails! At the same time, He never forces anyone to follow His plan. He always leaves the final decisions to us, and regretfully, we too often don't seek His plan and heed His advice.

But here's the Good News: It's not too late to get on track with His plan. If you haven't already done so, invite Jesus Christ into your heart; then renew your mind with His Word and spend some time daily seeking His wisdom and guidance.

Now, consider this: "For we are God's [own] handiwork (His workmanship), recreated in Christ Jesus, [born anew] that we may do those good works which God predestined (planned beforehand) for us [taking paths which He prepared ahead of time], that we should walk in them [living the good life which He prearranged and made ready for us to live]." *(Ephesians 2:10 AMP)*

It's a great plan!

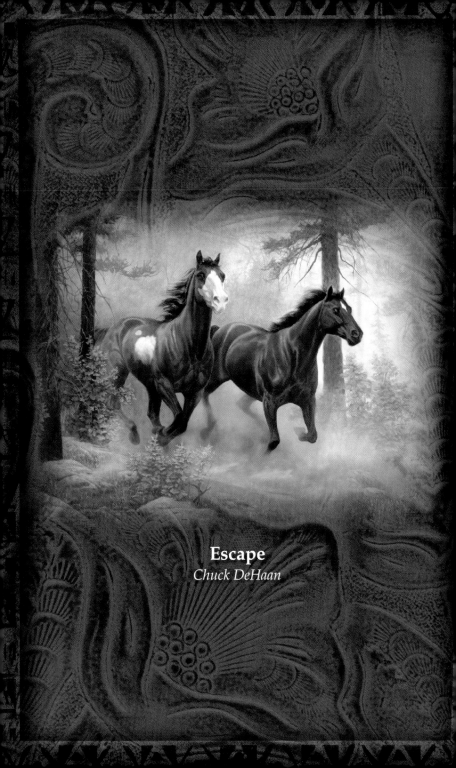

Escape
Chuck DeHaan

Habitual Forgiver

So that, on the contrary, you ought rather to forgive and comfort him, lest perhaps such a one be swallowed up with too much sorrow. Therefore I urge you to reaffirm your love to him. For to this end I also wrote, that I might put you to the test, whether you are obedient in all things. Now whom you forgive anything, I also forgive. For if indeed I have forgiven anything, I have forgiven that one for your sakes in the presence of Christ, lest Satan should take advantage of us; for we are not ignorant of his devices.
2 Corinthians 2:7-11

One habit the Lord never wants you to break is forgiveness . . . and if you don't have that habit, get it immediately!

Failure-to-forgive, resentment, and bitterness are open invitations the enemy uses to kill, steal from, and destroy anyone who harbors these emotions. Paul makes it clear in the scriptures above that Satan uses these devices against us. One of the best definitions I've heard on un-forgiveness – it's like swallowing a poisonous pill, thinking it will affect the other person!

So often when we are offended by someone, our emotions want to rise up in anger, retribution, and resentment. We want to "get back at them – after all, I've got a 'right' to feel this way after what they did to me!"

Jesus says to do exactly the opposite . . . pray for them, love them and above all, forgive them. You will live a longer, healthier, happier life for it. Be a habitual forgiver. Remember, you will never be called upon to bestow more forgiveness on anyone than God has already given you.

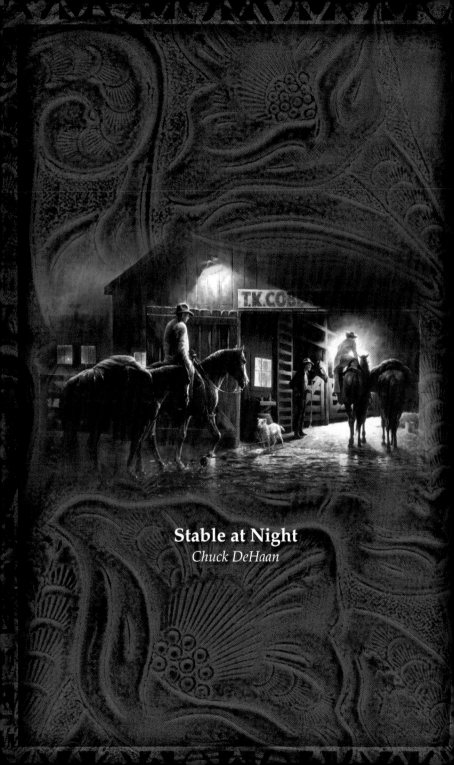

Stable at Night
Chuck DeHaan

Stakes Winner in the Barn

But you, beloved, building yourselves up on your most holy faith,
praying in the Holy Spirit, keep yourselves in the love of God,
looking for the mercy of our Lord Jesus Christ unto eternal life.
Jude 20, 21

E very believer has a stakes winner in his or her barn, but many never go to the entry booth with him.

That stakes winner is the Holy Spirit, and He came to live in you (in a measure) the moment you accepted Jesus Christ as your personal Savior. The disciples received that measure when Jesus (following His resurrection) breathed on them in *John 20:22.* Then some fifty days later on the Day of Pentecost, "they were all *filled* with the Holy Spirit and began to speak with other tongues as the Spirit gave them utterance." *(Acts 2:4, emphasis mine)*

When they spoke in tongues, they were speaking to God *(1 Corinthians 14:2)* – praying, and they were "praying in the Holy Spirit," as pointed out in our scripture above from Jude. Just look at the wonderful benefits of this type of praying: "building up your faith" and "keeping in the love of God!" How powerful and wonderful is that?

"But I don't know how to pray in tongues," someone will say. No problem . . . just ask for it. Look at *Luke 11:1,* "If you then, being evil, know how to give good gifts to your children, how much more will your heavenly Father give the Holy Spirit to those who ask Him!"

Some refer to speaking in tongues as their prayer language. The gift of tongues listed by Paul in *1 Corinthians 12:10* is for use in the congregation; the Apostle outlines in chapter fourteen the orderly use of this gift -- with interpretation -- during church services. But the personal prayer language is for *every* believer, a mighty spiritual tool to use, especially when we are not sure how to pray or intercede in our natural language. *(Romans 8:26, 27)*

So, get to the entry booth, believer! There's a sure-fire stakes winner in your barn (inside you), primed and ready to run.

Quality Time
Tim Cox

Love and Laughter

He who does not love does not know God, for God is love.
1 John 4:8

O ver the past eight to ten years I have at times received reminders from the Holy Spirit of how he wanted me to operate – *in love and laughter.* Those reminders generally came when I would have a tendency to take myself too seriously, or when a circumstance or situation would attempt to usher in some type of fear.

Whenever a believer begins to think that the success of the Kingdom of God depends on him or her . . . well, they're taking themselves entirely too seriously. Loosen up and laugh a little. After all, it's not your great ability, performance, or faith that's going to determine the final outcome – it's His!

So, relax, let go, and enjoy the journey. Certainly you need to be obedient to what God has called you to do, but He never intended it to be a burden to you.

And if any hint of fear tries to come upon you, shuck it off immediately. Fear is never God's modus operandi with a believer. Always keep *2 Timothy 1:7* in mind . . . "For God has not given us a spirit of fear, but of love, power, and a sound mind."

"But Chaplain," someone will say, "I learned so much from that fearful situation that happened to me; I just figured it was God's will for me." Wrong! God was the one who intervened and brought you the victory, but He's never the author of fear. Look at Jesus' own words in *John 10:10* . . . "The thief comes but to kill, steal and destroy. I have come that they may have life and life more abundantly."

Fear is not abundant living; rather it's most often a tactic of the enemy to rob you of your peace, faith, and the ultimate victory. But God is love, He operates in love, and "perfect love casts out fear." *(1 John 4:18)* So learn to laugh at the devil, laugh at fear, and laugh at contrary circumstances. Then walk in the love and power of God!

A Lot Like Heaven
Tim Cox

Enjoy

Command those who are rich in this present age not to be haughty, nor to trust in uncertain riches but in the living God, who gives us richly all things to enjoy.
I Timothy 6:17

"Enjoy," said the smiling young waitress as she set my delicious-looking chef salad in front of me and whisked away to her next table.

As I picked up my fork and aimed my first thrust, that same word – *Enjoy* – rose up on the inside of me in that wonderfully familiar, still-small Voice. Somehow, I knew He was referring to a whole lot more than this beautifully arranged dish of turkey, cheese, and garden vegetables . . . He was referring to my whole life.

Tonya, my oldest daughter, calls those type of words and incidents as "God kisses," little daily reminders of His bountiful blessings and unconditional love. "Thank you, Father," I responded. "I will, indeed, enjoy this salad, and I will continue to enjoy this wonderful walk in Your Kingdom that You have prepared for me."

As I chomped down on the lettuce and etceteras, my mind raced over the past few years as I had come to better understand the true nature of God (love) and the limitless benefits that He has provided for me in Christ Jesus. What a contrast it was to the pressures of the world and a regiment of religious traditions that had marked my life in earlier years.

In the scripture above we often center up on "not trusting in uncertain riches . . . ," but miss the *enjoyment* of all that God has given us. In some traditional circles of Christianity it has actually been considered sinful to enjoy things, and feelings, and money, and LIFE! Some of us have been taught that to be broke-down, beat-up, and "suffering for Jesus" is very spiritual. But is this what Jesus meant when he said in *John 10:10* "...I've come that you might have life and life more abundantly"?

When God created man and put him in the garden, He gave Adam every single thing that he would ever need . . . for his *enjoyment*. We all know that Adam blew the deal. But Jesus went to the cross and got it back for us. Our part is to believe that in our hearts . . . and *enjoy!*

. . . I've come that
you might have
life and life more
abundantly.

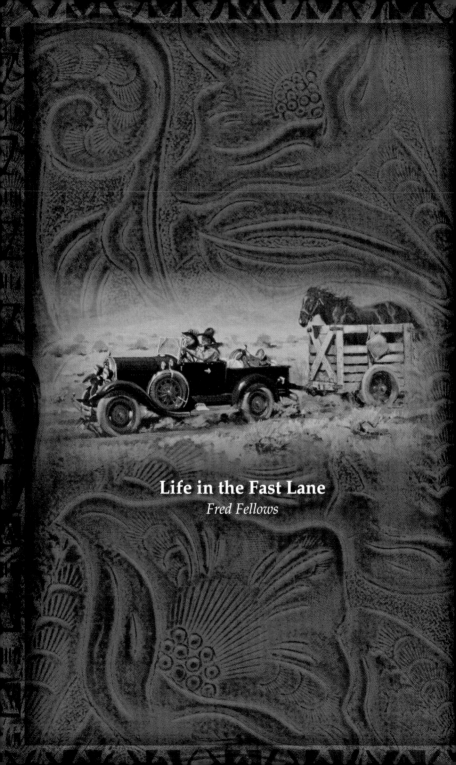

Life in the Fast Lane

Fred Fellows

Driving in Love

Let your gentleness be known to all men. The Lord is at hand. **Philippians 4:5**

A friend of mine once commented that one of the most noticeable changes in his life after being born again came in his driving. "Instead of being in such a hurry and often cutting in on people, I found myself looking for people to allow to cut in or go before me," he explained.

His comments convinced me to re-examine my own driving and how my old nemeses – impatience – sometimes weasels in during driving times. Am I really in that big of a hurry? Why not slow down and just enjoy the journey? Or simply get in the habit of leaving a little bit early?

All it takes is some planning, a little practice and (ouch!) a measure of discipline. Come to think of it, these principles can apply to many aspects of our lives. The love of God and it's manifestations are limitless . . . even in heavy traffic.

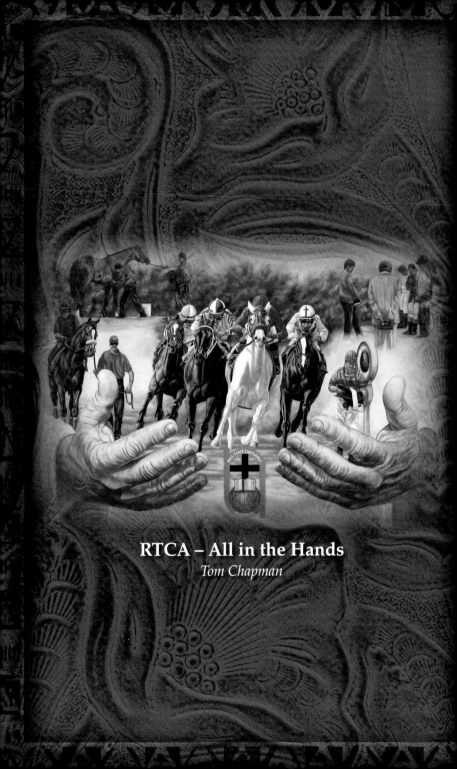

RTCA – All in the Hands

Tom Chapman

What Does God Think of Horse Racing?

For the eyes of the Lord run to and fro throughout the whole earth, to show Himself strong on behalf of those whose heart is loyal to Him. **2 Chronicles 16:9**

I get that question about horse racing occasionally, usually from some religious acquaintance who has little concept of the unconditional love of God and His immense interest in every facet of our lives.

Usually, my answer goes something like this: "He enjoys it! After all, it was His idea." That generally raises the religious hackles on the back of their necks, or just leaves them dumbfounded. But let me explain.

The Bible says "Every good and perfect gift is from above, and comes down from the Father of lights, with whom there is no variation or shadow of turning." *(James 1:17)* God created these beautiful, four-footed animals (by the way, they didn't evolve from some slimy critter that crawled out of the swamp eons ago) for the *enjoyment* of His man, who was the epitome of His creation.

It didn't take God by surprise the first time a couple of boys decided to find out whose mount could get to the water well first. Now that first race may well have been on donkeys, or even camels. But I'll give you pretty good odds that it didn't take long for them to figure out it was a whole lot more fun – and faster – on horseback.

I'll also wager that when God led the horse before Adam to see what he would name it, there was no tag around the animal's neck saying "Thou shalt not race, nor shalt thou enjoy." God knew exactly what was in store for this equine creation, and it was for a lot more than to simply be a beast of burden for His man.

Throughout the second chapter of Genesis, in which God reiterated the creation scene and re-emphasized that Adam was to "take dominion" over all the creatures, one gets the distinct impression that this whole endeavor was for the benefit and *enjoyment* (there's that word again) of man. Yet, most organized religion has done its best to convince us that life with God is dull, confining, and certainly not much fun. Nothing could be further from the truth. But that misconception is primarily the reason I personally spent the first 33 years of my life avoiding any real commitment to walk with Him.

Ironically, the "fun" I thought I was having resulted in a heart attack at the unseemly age of 30. Even after God (Who had nothing whatsoever to do with the heart attack – that was all my own doing) supernaturally spoke to me some two years later in the most loving way imaginable, I still refused to give up the sin and pressures in my life that were leading to sure destruction. I just knew He wanted to take away all my fun!

And I've got a pretty good notion that each of us either thinks that way, or did at one time in our life. On two different one-on-one conversations with trainers, I've had the Holy Spirit speak these words to me: "Tell him that if he will let Me be the Head Trainer, I'll lead him to heights he's not even dreamed of!"

Did that mean the trainer was going to win every race he entered? Probably not. Did it mean that his barn would be filled with nothing but Big Horses? Probably not. But I do think the Lord wanted to have a relationship with these guys (both were already believers) that would have taken them to a whole 'nother level, a place of enjoyment and peace in their profession and their lives they had never imagined.

To my knowledge, neither trainer took God up on His offer. Perhaps they were afraid God would take the fun out . . . not want them to handle things "their way."

But think about it – this is the Creator of the horse, the One Who knows it inside out . . . knows exactly how to get the very best out of that animal. And He wants to share it with you!

Someone will say, "Was God playing favorites with these guys?" Absolutely not. Just consider our lead scripture above from *2 Chronicles*. God is making that offer to let Him be the Head Trainer in the life of every trainer, every owner, every groom, every individual. In the gospel of Matthew, Jesus said, "Come to Me, all you who labor and are heavy laden, and I will give you rest. Take My yoke upon you and learn from me, for I am gentle and lowly in heart, and you will find rest for your souls. For my yoke is easy and My burden is light."   Now, look at how The Message Bible says this:

 "Are you tired? Worn out? Burned out on religion? Come to me. Get away with me and you'll recover your life. I'll show you how to take a real rest. Walk with me and work with me – watch how I do it. Learn the unforced rhythms of grace. I won't lay anything heavy or ill-fitting on you. Keep company with me and you'll learn to live freely and lightly."

How does God feel about horse racing?   He enjoys it. But more importantly, He loves you, and wants you to enjoy horse racing with Him.

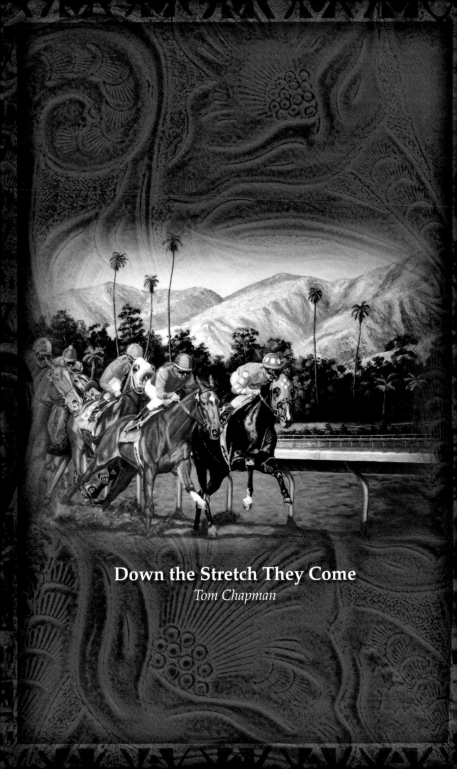

Down the Stretch They Come
Tom Chapman

Long Shots.

The Lord is not slack concerning His promise, as some count slackness, but is longsuffering toward us, not willing that any should perish but that all should come to repentance. II Peter 3:9

I love it when a long shot comes in. No, I don't bet on them; I just love to see an underdog in the winner's circle. And it happens most every day at the track in one race or another.

Every believer, every child of God was a long shot. Jesus said that there are *many* who go through the wide gate of destruction, but *few* who enter the narrow gate to everlasting life. *(Matthew 7:13-14)* So, we were long shots to make it – the odds were against us. Not that God doesn't desire that every man be saved, as our lead scripture above points out . . . it's God's perfect will that every human being come to a saving knowledge of the Lord Jesus Christ.

While we may be in a minority right now – according to Jesus' own words – we are on the brink of the greatest revival this world has ever seen. And the race track is right smack dab in the middle of it! As long shots are walking into the winner's circle at tracks every day, there are even more long shots entering daily into the Kingdom of God as the Lord pours out His spirit upon all flesh in these last days. *(Joel 2:28)*

The underdogs are coming in . . . you gotta love it!

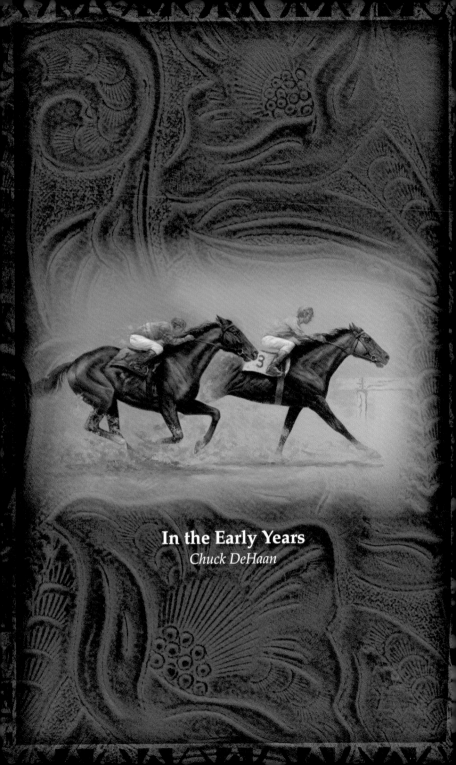

In the Early Years

Chuck DeHaan

Bits in Horses' Mouths

For we all stumble in many things. If anyone does not stumble in word, he is a perfect man, able also to bridle the whole body. Indeed, we put bits in horses' mouths that they may obey us, and we turn their whole body. Look also at ships: although they are so large and are driven by fierce winds, they are turned by a very small rudder wherever the pilot desires. Even so the tongue is a little member and boasts great things. See how great a forest a little fire kindles! **James 3:2-5**

James, the head of the church at Jerusalem and Jesus' natural brother, evidently had a little horse savvy when he penned the above verses in his letter to the twelve tribes of believers. We don't know if he had any riding experience, and most likely he didn't know the difference in high port, low port, spade, or snaffle bits, but James certainly had a handle on what keeps a half ton of horseflesh in control by its rider. More importantly, he gives us great comparisons of bridle bits and boat rudders with that most powerful little member of our body – the almighty tongue.

I recently heard a respected motivational speaker say, "You and I are the sum total today of all the thoughts we've had and the words we have spoken in our lifetimes . . . the tongue is what literally controls, dictates, and determines our very lives."

Those seem like overly strong statements, until you delve into God's word and see what He has to say about our words. Consider these scriptures:

"Death and life are in the power of the tongue, and those who love it will eat its fruit." *(Proverbs 18:21)*

"For as he [a man or woman] thinks in his heart, so is he." *(Proverbs 23:7)*

"For out of the abundance of the heart, the mouth speaks." *(Matthew 12:34)*

"Keep your heart with all diligence, for out of it spring the issues of life." *(Proverbs 4:23)*

Now, consider that God used words (faith-filled words) to speak the universe into existence. Then He created man in His own image, after which He instructed the man to "…have dominion over the fish of the sea, over the birds of the air, and over every living thing that moves on the earth." *(Genesis 1:28)* Man was to take that dominion through his ability to speak words.

Get the picture? The words we speak and the thoughts we have are so much more important than most of us have ever considered. Most probably, each of us could use a little "spade-bit application" to our tongues.

. . . the tongue
is what literally
controls, dictates,
and determines
our very lives.

Roping!
Chuck DeHaan

Faith or Presumption

For we are His workmanship, created in Christ Jesus for good works, which God prepared beforehand that we should walk in them. **Ephesians 2:10**

Several years ago the Lord spoke a plan to my heart that would be a source of great blessings for me and many others. I proceeded to make several plans (on paper), and then – based upon a particular circumstance – I took a "step of faith" in a certain action. However, my action fell flat on its face, a complete failure. While the actual damage was minimal, it left me quite disappointed and somewhat baffled. I went to the Lord with my predicament.

He answered me with one word: *"Presumption!"* As I meditated on His answer, I realized that I had acted on my own, based solely on a circumstance, without any instruction from Him. I had *presumed,* with no word or confirmation from the Holy Spirit. But, at least I was getting a good lesson in learning about faith verses presumption.

My wife and I had cut our spiritual teeth in the seventies on some wonderful faith messages, which totally turned our lives around. However, some of those messages were chocked full of formulas and methods which encouraged one to always "step out on your faith" – take action in order to receive from God. Then, one day I was reading about faith and works in the book of James: "Was not Abraham our father justified by works when he offered Isaac his son on the alter? Do you see that faith was working together with his works, and by works faith was made perfect?" *(James 2:21, 22)*

I vividly recall saying out loud, "But, Lord, that was something you spoke to Abraham to do!" He promptly answered me right back in my spirit, *"That's exactly right!"*

As I thought more on His answer, I realized that it took great faith for Abraham to be obedient to God in offering his son. Perhaps just as important, however, I began to see that God does not intend for us to manufacture these great works on our own. Instead, we are to learn to listen for His voice and His instruction in this walk of faith. Note in our scripture above: "which *God* prepared beforehand that we should walk in them." (emphasis mine)

About that same time another scripture came very alive to me: "But those who *wait* on the LORD shall renew their strength; they shall mount up with wings like eagles, they shall run and not be weary, they shall walk and not faint." *(Isaiah 40:31, emphasis mine)*

I'm convinced that God never intends our individual walks with Him to be difficult and full of failures, but rather journeys of victory, full of love, peace, joy, faith, and obedience . . . not presumption.

. . . we are to learn
to listen for His
voice and His
instruction in this
walk of faith.

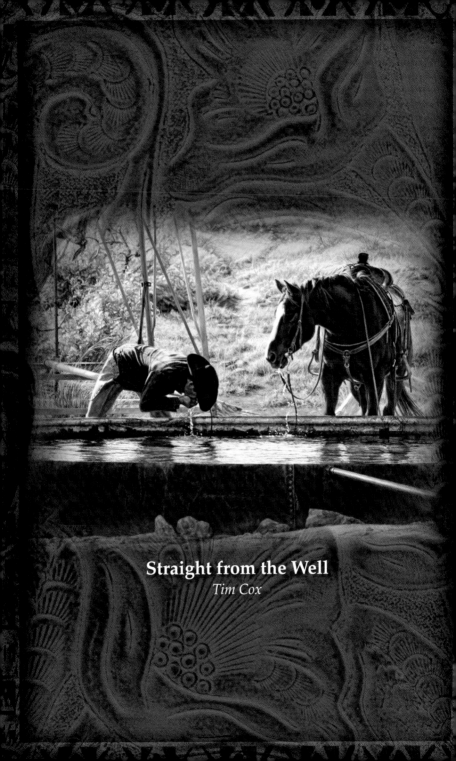

Straight from the Well
Tim Cox

More, Much More

...that if you confess with your mouth the Lord Jesus and believe in your heart that God has raised Him from the dead, you will be saved. **Romans 10:9**

Since I can remember, as a believer, this passage in Romans has been used to lead individuals into their born-again experience, "saving" them from eternal damnation and the judgment of God. But the Apostle Paul, when he penned these words to the believers in Rome, never intended the experience to end there, i.e., saved from the fires of hell.

The Greek word Paul used for saved, *sozo,* entails much more than simply obtaining our "fire insurance." Sozo includes safety and protection, health and healing, deliverance from oppression, as well as peace, provision, and prosperity in every area. That's the total-package salvation that Jesus Christ obtained for us through his death, burial, and resurrection. And this is what the Lord Jesus Himself meant when He stated in *John 10:10,* "I have come that they may have life, and that they may have it *more abundantly."* (emphasis mine)

Jesus paid a gargantuan price (so big that few, if any, of us can get our minds wrapped around it) for us to have and enjoy the abundant life. Yes, indeed, we'll have trials and tribulations, as well as persecutions for the Word's sake; Jesus said that. Then He added, "But take heart! I've conquered the world." *(John 16:33 The Message)*

He conquered it for you and me! Get that settled in your heart. When you do, you will start experiencing that abundant life of health, wealth, peace, and fullness that belong to you.

Winter Renegade
Chuck DeHaan

Underserved

For by grace you have been saved through faith, and that not of yourselves; it is the gift of God, not of works, lest anyone should boast. **Ephesians 2:8, 9**

Prayed for a man in the hospital a few years ago who had just been operated on for cancer. In our visit he shared with me that he had accepted Jesus as his Savior and been baptized as a teenager . . . "but hadn't done a very good job of being a Christian for the last several years."

I strongly sensed he was saying in his heart that "he really couldn't expect the Lord to heal him, with his poor performance as a believer – he simply didn't deserve it."

I explained to him that Jesus was his Healer as well as his Savior, and that his healing would come the same way his salvation did – strictly by grace through faith, with nothing whatsoever to do with his performance or works.

Consternation appeared on his face as he tried to digest the spiritual bombshell I had just dropped on his religion. I understood exactly what he was thinking because I operated under this same theology several years ago, as have many Christians today. A great deal of organized religion has led us to believe that God's system operates under a different guideline once we're born again . . . that we somehow slip back under the law and can qualify for His blessings only if we keep all the rules and do all the good stuff for Him.

Religion has a way of concentrating on *doing* rather than being . . . on rules rather than relationship. Consequently, just like my friend in the hospital, we often burn out on the religious system and go our own way, seldom realizing that we are missing out on the greatest life imaginable – a close, loving, one-on-One with our Creator, who so desires this tight relationship with us.

But nobody deserved it. That's why Jesus went to the cross; hence, we're no longer the undeserved.

Cattle Drive
Chuck DeHaan

Holy Rollers

Roll your works upon the Lord [commit and trust them wholly to Him; He will cause your thoughts to become agreeable to His will, and] so shall your plans be established and succeed.
Proverbs 16:3 AMP

As a young boy growing up on a ranch in central Texas, I remember hearing kids on the school bus making fun of a little rock church on the river where the "holy rollers" congregated. When I quizzed my bus companions on what they meant, the answer was, "Oh, they all lie down on the floor and roll in the aisles during church."

The answer made little sense to this young Methodist, but somehow it stuck with me. Some thirty-plus years later, I found myself pastor of a small charismatic church where it was not uncommon for someone to be "slain in the spirit." I never cared much for that term, but it describes someone being touched by the Holy Spirit and suddenly *falling out* on the floor; usually it lasted for only a minute or so, although I've known some to *stay out* for an hour or more. Many wonderful testimonies and words from the Lord have come from those encounters with the Holy Spirit.

Then, one day I recalled the little rock church on the river, realizing I was now one of 'em -- a holy roller! Not long afterwards, my wife, who had conducted a ladies Bible study even prior to the opening of our church, received a word from the Holy Spirit in her study time. "I want to show you what a true *holy* roller is," and He directed her to the scripture above in the Amplified Bible, the translation she has always used.

Turns out that God's *holy roller* is actually a wholly roller! This scripture has since become one of the keys that we've lived our lives around. It involves commitment, trust, and hearing God's voice in your thoughts . . . and it works.

Paint in the Mist
Chuck DeHaan

Unchangeable Lord

Every good and perfect gift is from above, and comes down from the Father of lights, with whom there is no variation or shadow of turning. **James 1:17**

"He's still doing the things He always did . . . He's an unchangeable Lord." So goes a line from a gospel song written and recorded by Psalmist and Pastor David Ingles on one of his many albums that bless the body of Christ.

The writer of Hebrews confirmed the Lord's unchangeableness when he stated "Jesus Christ is the same yesterday, today and forever." *(Hebrews 13:8)* And that is exactly what the Apostle James is telling us in the scripture above. Father God, whom Jesus copied in everything He said and did, has not changed one iota from all the love and miracles He handed out some 2,000 years ago when Jesus had His earthly ministry.

When we believers let the Holy Spirit settle this in our hearts, He can work the same miracles through us as He did through Jesus. Remember, He's an *unchangeable Lord.*

Blizzard Peril

Chuck DeHaan

"Lord, be with us."

"And when you pray, do not use vain repetitions as the heathen do, for they think that they will be heard for their many words. **Matthew 6:7**

I've prayed it; and you've most likely prayed it, because ninety-nine percent of all professing Christians have prayed "Lord, be with us," at one time or another. Yet, it is a prayer of doubt and unbelief, a prayer that is in direct conflict with God's Word; therefore, a prayer He cannot answer!

Hebrews 13:5 quotes God's promise in the Old Covenant *(Deut. 31:6, 8),* "He will not leave you nor forsake you." Under the New Covenant, when we are born again, the Holy Spirit comes to dwell with us and, in fact, lives in us. *(John 14:17)* Hence, when we pray "Lord, be with us," we are denying that He's already there, or we're actually confessing that he has *left* us.

"But it sounds so good . . . so righteous. . . so religious," you will say. And that's a big part of the problem — it's religious rhetoric, and Jesus was quite definite about avoiding that very thing, as pointed out in our lead scripture above.

If you're really "hung up" on this old phrase, turn it into a praise, rather than a petition . . . "Lord, thank you for always being with me, for never leaving me, and for always hearing my prayer!" Let's be scriptural and accurate in our prayer life. We're not out to be religious . . . we're out to get results!

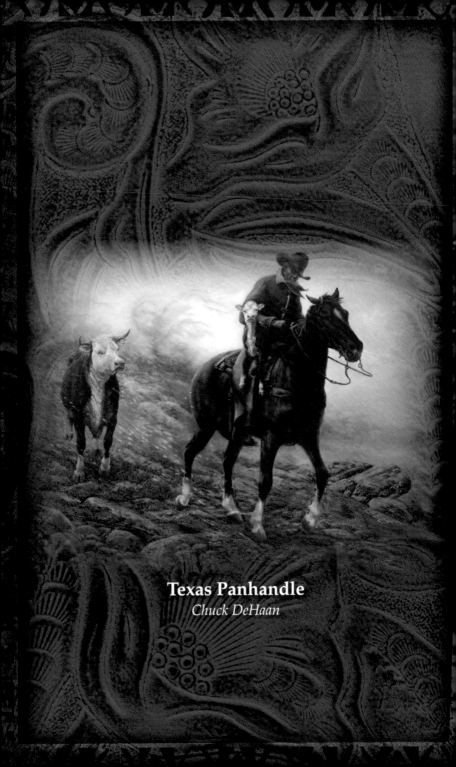

Texas Panhandle
Chuck DeHaan

But Would He Do It for Me?

"Therefore I say to you, whatever things you ask when you pray, believe that you receive them, and you will have them."
Mark 11:24

That's a question that has probably popped into the mind of every believer at one time or another concerning God answering a prayer. Perhaps it was a prayer for a healing in your body, or a financial need, or protection in a precarious or dangerous situation . . . maybe a prayer for wisdom in an important decision.

You knew that God had the ability and power to answer that prayer and meet the need. You had read about Him doing it in the Bible, and maybe you had heard testimonies of others having that particular prayer answered. "But would He do it for me?"

Whenever that thought comes up, get rid of it immediately! It's either straight from the devil, or it's a product of an erroneous, self-righteous attitude. Either way, you need to apply *2 Corinthians 10:5* – "casting down arguments and every high thing that exalts itself against the knowledge of God, bringing every thought into captivity to the obedience of Christ . . ."

The truth is, God has already made full provision and answered your prayer. Your part is to simply believe it and receive it. Note our lead scripture from the gospel of Mark. For confirmation, look at these scriptures pertaining to those prayer requests in the first paragraph above:

"He Himself took our infirmities and bore our sicknesses." *(Matt. 8:17);* "by whose stripes you were healed. *(I Peter 2:24b);* "For you know the grace of our Lord Jesus Christ, that though He was rich, yet for your sakes He became poor, that you through His poverty might become rich." *(2 Corinthians 8:9);* "For He Himself has said, "I will never leave you nor forsake you." *(Hebrews 13:5);* "If any of you lacks wisdom, let him ask of God, who gives to all liberally and without reproach, and it will be given to him." *(James 1:5)*

Yes, indeed, He will do it for you. He already has!

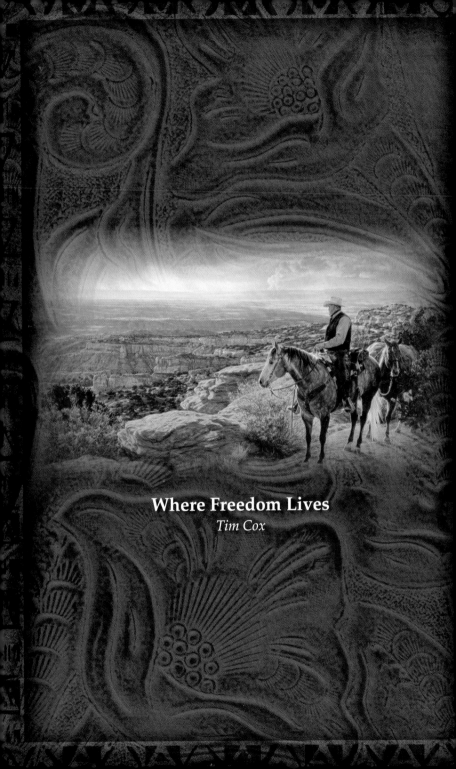

Where Freedom Lives
Tim Cox

The Praise Privilege

For though we walk in the flesh, we do not war according to the flesh. For the weapons of our warfare are not carnal but mighty in God for pulling down strongholds, casting down arguments and every high thing that exalts itself against the knowledge of God, bringing every thought into captivity to the obedience of Christ. **2 Corinthians 10:3-5**

We are in a spiritual battle. The Apostle Paul makes this very clear in the statements above that he wrote to the church at Corinth, as well as those he scribed to the church at Ephesus: "For we do not wrestle against flesh and blood, but against principalities, against powers, against the rulers of darkness of this age, against spiritual hosts of wickedness in the heavenly places." (*Ephesians 6:12*)

Paul goes on to explain putting on the whole armor of God, which includes your waist girded with truth, the breastplate of righteousness, feet shod with preparation of the gospel of peace, shield of faith, helmet of salvation, sword of the spirit (God's Word), and praying in the spirit.

One weapon – actually a vehicle – which incorporates our full armor is praise; it can be one of the most effective ways of putting the enemy on the run . . . "Resist the devil and he will flee from you." (*James 4:7*) Resist is an active verb, not a passive one. When we began to praise the Lord in the midst of a trial, temptation, or contrary circumstance, we (in football terms) suddenly take an *offensive* position rather than a *defensive* one. And continual praise will take us right into the end zone for a score!

Every prayer we utter should began with praise and thanks. There's something about praise that not only evokes the angels of God into action on our behalf, but activates the forces of faith, hope, and joy on the inside of us.

Praise is a powerful privilege at our complete command. Don't neglect it.

Shallow Crossing
Jack Sorenson

Fording the Stream

A man who has friends must himself be friendly, but there is a friend who sticks closer than a brother.
Proverbs 18:24

"He'll do to swim the river with?"

It was a phrase I sometimes heard as a youngster growing up on ranches in central and east Texas. Actually, in cowboy terms, it was one of the highest compliments you could pay someone. It meant that this was a person you could depend upon to stay with you when the going got rough – someone who would "stick with you and see you through to the end."

As a five-year-old living in Coryell County outside Gatesville, TX, I once had occasion to apply that phrase to a horse. Dad and I had saddled up at the barn to go check on a herd of sheep that was kept in a pasture about a half-mile away. I was on my half-Shetland, Tony (about 13 hands tall), and Dad was riding Scooter, a race-bred Quarter Horse gelding that stood about 15-2.

On the way to the sheep pasture we forded little Bee House Creek, which was about ankle deep to the horses at the gravel bar we crossed. However, at some point, while we were checking on the sheep, a very unusual flash flood came rushing down the creek, and when we headed back home we were confronted with a roaring, muddy stream, probably some six to seven feet deep at our crossing.

After surveying the situation, Dad swung me up behind him on Scooter with instructions to "hang on tight," which I readily heeded, while at the same time holding Tony's reins in one hand. Dad coaxed Scooter into the muddy stream and we headed across.

I well remember feeling Scooter's strong swimming strokes under me as we made our way safely to the other side. But

Tony's strokes weren't near as stout, and after jerking the reins from my hand, he finally made it across, some thirty or forty yards downstream from us. Ol' Scooter definitely earned the cowboy homage that day . . . "he'll do to swim the river with!"

Most all of us have had a friend or two that would stick with us through trying times and help us "get to the other side of the creek." And, regretfully, most of us have also had some disappointments along that line. The Proverb above, however, is about a special kind of friend.

That *friend* is the Lord Jesus Christ, and He is a man of His word. When He says "I'll never leave you nor forsake you," He stands behind it. If you don't already – get to know Him . . . "He'll do to swim the river with!"

Sam Ed Spence, age 5, on his first horse, Tony, 1944.

That *friend* is the
Lord Jesus Christ,
and He is a man
of His word.

Barnward Bound
Tom Chapman

Teaching an Old Horse New Tricks

"Take my yoke upon you and learn from Me, for I am gentle and lowly in heart, and you will find rest for your souls." **Matthew 11:29**

J ust about the time I think I've got this race of life figured out…WHAM-O…along comes a whole new condition book. I thought I'd gotten into black-type country, when in reality I had barely stepped onto the track! Sometimes the Lord's sense of humor sorta overwhelms me in this area . . . like when He says, "You know, son, you're just getting started good – you're a long way from arriving!"

But when you think about it, that's what makes being a Christian exciting. It just never gets boring with Jesus! I have found that when I get quiet and really open up my soul to Him and His way of thinking, then tremendous possibilities and exciting plans begin to unfold before me.

And remember, God's Word says that He is "no respecter of persons." That means He doesn't love me any more than He loves you. He shows no partiality. He doesn't take sides, or exhibit bias, favoritism, or discrimination. While society (the world) makes distinctions among people, God's love and grace are available for all and can be received by anyone.

I think a big key here is simply slowing down long enough and tuning in to the Holy Spirit, the One who lives on the inside of every believer who has accepted Jesus Christ as his or her personal Savior. The society we live in and the culture most of us have been reared in is not conducive to turning the reins over to the Lord and allowing Him to direct our steps *(Proverbs 3:6)* . . . putting us on the track that *He* wants us to run on.

Someone said, "Why, Chaplain, if I do that He might take all my goodies away from me, and send me off as a destitute missionary to somewhere they don't even have horses, much less fast horses!"

First off, let me assure you, God is a *giver*, not a *taker*. He wants to give you the desires of your heart -- desires of wholeness, wellness, peace, and plenty. All He wants to *take* from you is your stress, anxiety, disease, infirmity, and lack. In fact, Jesus has already provided all of that for us through His death and resurrection via the cross. But to receive it, we have to believe it; it's called faith.

Dive into His word, find out for yourself. Take Jesus' advice from our lead scripture above in Matthew. Finding His true rest for our souls is a great place for an old horse to learn a new trick or two.

God wants to give
you the desires of
your heart.

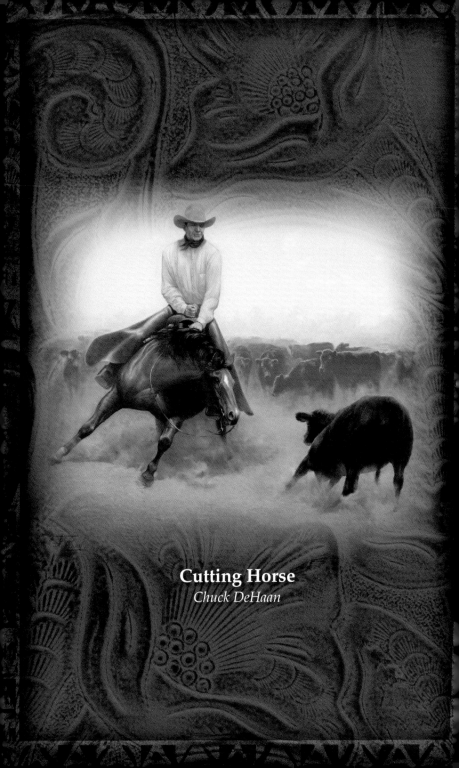

Cutting Horse
Chuck DeHaan

Live slow...
but ride a fast horse

". . . , I have come that they may have life , and that they may have it more abundantly." **John 10:10**

A few years ago Fairgrounds Chaplain Waverly Parsons (he was at Trinity Meadows at that time) gave me a pretty, stained cedar board with the words above burned into it. Actually, he donated the piece of art for a prize in our spring chaplaincy golf tournament. But I was so impressed with the message and the quality of his work that I hung it in my office (where it remains today), and substituted a contribution of my own to the tournament prize list.

At 74, I'm finally learning to take Waverly's cedar-board advice. Somebody say, "It's about time, Chaplain!" I'm sure that I've got some years on at least ninety per cent of the folks reading this, so I want to pass on some good advice, regardless of your age – SLOW DOWN!

Don't just "take time to stop and smell the roses" . . . reflect on their beauty, thank Jesus for them, then buy a few and take 'em home to mama as an invitation for a quiet meal together.

As a veteran (and co-instigator) of a broken marriage at 27, a heart attack at 30 and a failed business at 38, I can testify to the senselessness of the fast-paced, worry-burdened, stress-filled, get-it-all-at-any-cost life that the world has to offer. Certainly there were a number of factors that contributed to my various downfalls, but a faulty priority attitude headed up the list.

Even after inviting Jesus Christ back into my life at age 33 and then accepting Him as my spirit-baptizer at 36, it still took me a while to slow down my breakneck pace, *really* put Him first place, and start enjoying the abundant life He tells us about in our scripture above. As I slowly responded to Jesus' teaching to quit worrying, take a day at a time, and get plenty of rest, the quality of my life vastly improved.

Problems? You bet…I still had some, still do today. But I learned that every problem didn't have to be solved in one day, and that if I *truly* trusted the Lord, He always took care of them in ways that often I hadn't even dreamed of! Most of the time it was simply a process of slowing down and learning to listen.

Proverbs 16:3 in the Amplified Bible says "Roll your works upon the Lord [commit and trust them wholly to Him; He will cause your thoughts to become agreeable to His will, and] so shall your plans be established and succeed." When I got hold of that scripture in my heart . . . well, that's when I became a true wholly roller. Today, I'm healthy, totally out of debt, and absolutely enjoying this journey.

And, incidentally, I also ride a very fast horse -- an eight-year-old Quarter mare that's carried me to several wins in ranch sorting and team penning.

So, slow down and get on the Jesus program of abundant living.

Roll your works
upon the Lord,
commit and trust
them wholly to
Him.

The Winner
Chuck DeHaan

The Drop

That if you confess with your mouth the Lord Jesus and believe in your heart that God raised Him from the dead, you will be saved. **Romans 10:9**

Possibly the most important part of our lead scripture above is "believe in your heart." Note it did *not* say, "believe in your head" . . . big, big difference.

A lot of folks have a head-knowledge of God, but don't know Him in their hearts. That's what the Apostle James was talking about when he said, "You believe there is one God. You do well. Even the demons believe – and tremble!" *(James 2:19)* Demons believe in God, but they have no heart capability as you and I do.

It's imperative that we make that "18-inch drop" from the head to the heart in order to experience God. It starts – as our scripture points out – by saying it with your mouth. You can use the following prayer to insure that you've made the drop:

Father God,
I ask you to forgive me of all my sins, shortcomings, and blown turns. I believe in my heart that Jesus Christ is your Son and that You raised Him from the dead. Lord Jesus, come into my heart; I receive You as the Lord of my life. AMEN